Board

The names of certain people in this book have been changed
to preserve privacy.
Published by Fledgling Press, 2015
Cover Design: Michael O'Shea
www.owenoshea.com/

www.fledglingpress.co.uk

Printed and bound by:
Bell and Bain, Glasgow

ISBN: 9781905916931

For Shona and David

ACKNOWLEDGEMENTS

My wife and best friend Shona for her love and unwavering support. She bought the boards and in doing so allowed me to find myself. She's also witnessed the less positive consequences of board ownership, without ever suggesting I give it all up for something more befitting a man of my years. She is my rock.

My wonderful son David. Having him beside me out at sea, in the skatepark, or up in the mountains, sharing adventures and just enjoying living in the moment together, has completed the circle. He's also due a special mention for taking many of the photographs in Board.

My mother Ena – 'the sea's the master' – for her support to my family over the years.

Mark 'Too Deep' Feeney for his friendship, boundless energy, infectious enthusiasm and occasional medical treatment. I wish him and Jen much love and happiness for their future together and look forward to the day when he joins me again at the Bay of Skaill.

Clare Cain at Fledgling Press for believing in Board and guiding it into print, and designer Michael O'Shea for producing the perfect cover.

Thurso legend Andy Bain for starting me, properly, down the surfer's path and for arranging the shaping of my beloved board. Should anyone reading this book decide they'd like to learn to surf, he's your man.

All the Orkney surfers, past and present, for never complaining about my ineptitude in the water.

The Edinburgh longboard skate pioneers, Neil Davey, Douglas Brown and Stephen Cairns for sharing The Stoke, and all of the Glasgow crew who welcomed me into their world at Kelvingrove.

Michael Brooke at Concrete Wave magazine for running with the original MacStoke road trip idea all those years back.

Author, journalist and surfer Alex Wade for his advice and cover quote.

Orkney author, storyteller and historian Tom Muir for his encouragement and advice.

David Gray and Myrid Ramsay for their friendship and support. I must also thank David for his work on some of the photographs in this book.

Finally, I'd like to express my gratitude to everyone who buys a copy of Board. I hope you enjoy my story. If it inspires you to go and try something new, find some inner peace, or just stick two fingers up to convention, I'll be very happy indeed.

INTRODUCTION

I'm standing on a rocky finger of coastline, looking out across the expanse of the Mediterranean. It's the height of the July day and the temperature in St Raphael has climbed into the 90s. Intense, broiling sunlight plays across the surface of the rather murky water, while a few feet below me gentle waves lap the base of my vantage point. The small beach to my right is packed with sunbathers, amongst them my three friends.

This is the first day of our week's holiday on the French Riviera. Having graduated in journalism two years previously, we're all now employed as junior reporters in Scotland. My three friends work urban beats in and around the city of Glasgow, whereas I work on the local weekly newspaper in my island home of Orkney. As such, I'm the only one who lives close to the ocean. I see and smell it every day and regularly travel across it on a ferry. I come from a long line of seafarers and my blood should be slightly saline. But my nautical genes are about to prove utterly worthless.

I've clambered onto the outcrop with the intention of diving dramatically into the water. Already badly sunburned, I'm wearing only a pair of skimpy Speedo swimming trunks and have equipped myself with a cheap mask and snorkel set, picked up for a few francs in the campsite shop.

My feet are shod in a pair of turquoise blue rubber water shoes, two sizes too small. They were the only beach footwear available in the shop, look like knobbly condoms and are agonisingly uncomfortable. I'd bought them earlier in the day after discovering how painful it was to walk on the rocky shoreline.

My friends watch from the beach with feigned interest as I pose for a few seconds, scanning the horizon in a moody kind of way. I think I look quite cool in my ridiculous shoes, tiny trunks and toy diving gear, but I'm pink and peeling on the outside and terrified on the inside.

Despite being surrounded by the sea back home, I've never actually dived into it before and the prospect is daunting. There's no going back though. Two of my friends are women, so ego dictates I follow through on my plan to expertly plunge like an arrow into the depths of the Med.

Thankfully I can actually swim a little, though my technique is high on effort and low on finesse. Having spent much of my late teens and early 20s lifting weights, I'm not the most buoyant of individuals and have been officially classed as 'one of life's sinkers' by a bemused swimming coach.

My stomach – tightly flexed for the benefit of my female audience – is churning. The water looks deep enough to accommodate someone of my size and weight hitting it at speed, but I feel as if I'm about to step onto the surface of the moon in nothing but my underpants, such is the alien nature of the ocean environment. I pull my mask and snorkel down over my face, take a deep, plastic-tainted breath and dive in.

From this modest height there's not enough time to straighten out my body and I smack the water with my stomach. The mask and snorkel come off my face and relocate around my neck. Completely disorientated and with my eyes screwed tightly shut, I pull hard for where I think the surface is and emerge gasping and spluttering into the light.

A huge German Shepherd dog suddenly appears on the rocks above me, barks and dives into the water. It paddles towards me as a small wave slaps my body against the rocky outcrop. I feel something stabbing at my knees and panic rises in my chest. I'm blowing hard and scrambling to get a grip on the rocks to pull myself out, but the backwash sucks me away towards North Africa.

Another wave surges into the channel and slams me back onto the rocks. The dog, its French owner bellowing and swearing at it from the shore, is still barking and swimming around in circles behind me. I'm not sure whether it's some official canine rescue effort or just an attempt at play.

More ocean surges into the channel and I'm lifted high enough to grab a better handhold on the rocks. I haul myself out of the waves and fall onto my knees. My ill-fitting rubber shoes ping off my feet simultaneously and drop into the water below. The barking dog grabs one in its mouth and swims off towards the beach.

Trying to compose myself, I look down at my knees, which now resemble pincushions. Black urchin spines are embedded beneath the skin and blood is starting to mix with the seawater, sun cream and sweat running down my shins. My pride is seriously wounded, but I make light of my injuries to my friends and spend the remainder of the day baking and peeling further in the sun, while pulling urchin spines from my knees with a pair of tiny plastic tweezers.

My worries about dying from urchin poisoning are superseded at night by the worst bout of diarrhoea I've ever had in my 25 years, my backside violently unloading whatever waterborne guests I'd swallowed earlier in the day. If, at this point in my life, someone had suggested I learn to surf, I would have laughed long and hard.

That trip to the South of France in 1992 pretty much confirmed everything I'd suspected about the ocean. It was beautiful to look at, but scary, moody and unpredictable.

After I returned home that summer, I went back to pursuing mildly risky land-based sports and feeding my passion for aviation. The early 90s had seen me qualify as a private pilot and, when I wasn't walking in the Scottish mountains, I was flying over them in a light aircraft. I was comfortable in the sky and competent in hostile mountain terrain, but the sea represented a final frontier I wasn't sure I wanted to cross.

Aside from trips to local beaches with the dog, I had little direct contact with the ocean again until 1996. On a winter holiday to the Algarve with my wife Shona, I watched two bodyboarders in wetsuits and fins jump off a pier into a raging sea. It seemed like suicide.

I simply had no frame of reference for an action like that. I'd spent a lot of time in the mountains and had a very clear idea of where my limitations lay in terms of the weather conditions I was prepared to venture out in.

Equally, aviation had a rigid framework of rules and procedures. One planned, checked, checked again and practiced continually for the statistically unlikely day when the propeller stopped turning, or the engine burst into flames.

Watching those bodyboarders leap off the pier into a thundering and relentless aquatic maelstrom, I didn't believe I could ever possess sufficient knowledge of the sea to allow me to do something like that safely. I thought it was merely blind confidence, or a death wish.

But, I also saw the appeal. Riding prone on their short bodyboards, the young Portuguese guys shot across the face of the waves at an amazing speed, with some performing 360-degree spins along the way. Once they'd completed their rides, they'd either paddle back out to sea or exit the water and come running along the pier to jump back in. It all seemed so breathtakingly audacious.

A few days later, once the sea had calmed down, I waded into the shallows at the same beach with the intention of trying to tap into some of what those guys had experienced. It was sunny and the water was warm. But the power contained in the moderately-sized waves astonished me.

Within minutes of leaving the shore I was knocked flat on my back by a chest-high wave and rolled onto the beach to think again. The mental shift from pleasure to blind panic was instantaneous and transported me back to the dog and urchin day in the South of France. I'd had some shaky moments in aircraft – making seat of the pants approaches in bad weather, or getting low on fuel, but this rapid, unexpected assault at the hands of the ocean completely overloaded my senses. There was absolutely nothing I could do about it.

Again, people were watching me, so I composed myself and went in for another round only to get washed by a heaving green wave onto an unseen cluster of urchin-covered rocks. I had to visit a medical clinic to have the spines removed from my feet and hands by an impatient doctor who'd seen it all before. There was definitely a pattern emerging in terms of my relationship with the sea and you'd have thought, this time, I might just have taken the hint.

Surprisingly, it was against this backdrop that I decided to learn to surf. Whilst my fingers had been burned by the sea – and punctured by its inhabitants – I had a strong sense of there being unfinished business to take care of. My desire to learn to surf was only partly to do with conquering an environment that scared me. My limited experiences so far – and my ancestral connection to the sea – had taught me that butting heads with it would spell certain death. But my fear of the ocean and my ineptitude within it frustrated me.

Looking out across the sea, whether in France, Portugal or at home, I knew the ocean possessed life-changing, as well as life-ending, potential. And surfing, from what I'd seen of it and its exponents, seemed to represent the ultimate expression of a harmonious relationship with this fluid environment. Surfers apparently respected and understood the sea, but they also had the confidence to work with it to their advantage. I just wanted to take a peek through the door into their realm and perhaps absorb some of what they had found.

Hobbling around the Algarve resort of Albufeira with bandaged toes and fingers, I went into a surfy-looking shop and bought a couple of surf brand t-shirts, a wallet and a pair of blue Vans skate trainers. There were pictures on the wall of the shop of barrelling turquoise waves and cool, smiling, bleached blonde pro-surfers.

I quite liked all the associated clothing and wanted, rather sadly in reflection, to buy into the whole beach lifestyle thing then and there. Seeing the blue Vans had also triggered off some very distant memory about skateboarding in the 70s and they seemed appropriate footwear for someone planning to learn to surf. I left the shop armed with what I thought were the basic tools needed for my reinvention as a surfer.

It's worth stating here and now that I didn't take up surfing because I wanted to write a book. As a journalist I briefly – and rather naively – harboured some vague idea about creating a surfing instruction manual for older beginners, once I had the sport mastered. But I'll never be good enough to tell other people, of any age, how they should catch waves. I can still barely catch them myself.

In the end almost 10 years were to pass after that Portuguese revelation before I found myself on a surfboard. By then I was approaching 40 and unaware of how hard the journey ahead would be.

CHAPTER 1

My pick up has been scheduled for 9.15am. I've arranged to be collected from outside a reception building in the centre of the large timeshare resort I'm staying in with Shona and our young son David. I have a rental car and map and would happily have driven the 40 miles north to the beach used by the surf school. However, they've insisted on coming to get me. It's only 8.30am, so I've plenty of time to reflect on the fact I'm finally about to learn to surf.

I haven't been in the sea since the Portuguese trip of 1996 and it's now July 2005. In the intervening period, I've acquired even more of surfing's lifestyle accoutrements – t-shirts, board shorts, magazines, flip-flops, wallets and key rings. But I've never actually laid my hands on a surfboard. It's a glaring omission in my master plan, but the need to learn to surf has been reduced by the demands of work and parenthood to a kind of distant background noise in my life.

However, when the chance to use a relative's timeshare apartment on the island of Fuerteventura arises – and I learn that this is a place with abundant waves – I again find my thoughts turning to surfing. This will be our first family holiday abroad, though, and I'm conscious that drowning would ruin it.

Ever supportive and patient, Shona buys me a 90 euro beginner's package as a 38th birthday present from a surf school on the island. Every day since then I've been on their website trying to imagine what fate awaits me in the Canaries.

According to the website, my three-day immersion in the technicalities of surfing will get me on my feet and riding waves in no time at all. I'll also learn about wave selection, safety and a load of other exotic stuff aimed at making me a confident waterman. I'm excited and, remembering my previous experiences in the sea, more than a little nervous.

Sitting on the steps of the resort's reception building, I open my rucksack and pull out copies of the emails I've been exchanging with the surf school in the lead-up to my arrival on the island. I unfold them repeatedly and double check the time and place for collection, as if they were some kind of insurance policy, or tangible proof that my dream is about to come true.

The pick-up time comes and goes, but I'm on holiday and pretending to be cool. In my head I'm now very nearly a surfer. Getting uptight about bad timekeeping is no longer appropriate behaviour.

An hour passes and I'm still waiting, my veneer of cool and relaxed wannabe surfer starting to peel away. It's getting warmer and the streets of the resort are much busier. The people in the reception area are now taking more interest in me, clearly wondering why I've been sitting for over an hour on their steps, staring at sheets of paper. I study the emails with a new intensity, and theatrically look at my watch a lot in an attempt to reassure them I'm not a criminal or suicide bomber.

A shirtless blonde guy in tatty blue board shorts suddenly appears in the street below me and runs up the steps. Barefoot, he's out of breath and clutching a crumpled sheet of paper.

"Surfing?" he asks sheepishly.

I nod.

"Yeah. Cool," he says, introducing himself as Alex and apologising profusely about the delay in picking me up. "Man! Finding your way around this place is a nightmare!"

Aged about 24, his accent is English, though the exact county of origin is impossible to detect as his voice has a languid, mid-Atlantic drawl to it. His distaste for the resort is obvious. I want to tell him I'm only staying there because I got the accommodation for free and I'm actually quite a cool, worldly kind of guy who would rather be sleeping in a battered VW camper van than this four-star place with its own pool, restaurant and children's entertainer.

At least he looks the part, or what I think is the part. The sides of his head have been shaved, leaving a floppy, sun-bleached blonde section of hair on top. He trots ahead of me, taking several wrong turnings through the resort's lanes, before we arrive at a dust-coated white minibus sporting some tired blue and yellow surfing graphics.

"I've got more people to collect from this place," he says, waving his hand disparagingly at the tightly-packed resort apartments and villas. "We're not down here much."

The minibus' clunky diesel engine fires up and we're on our way. I sit up front beside Alex and we spend the next 20 minutes looking for more customers for the school. He drives with one hand while scanning his sheet of paper, trying to relate the information on it to the Spanish street and hotel names.

We go up and down a series of narrow side streets and finally spot an unhappy-looking couple sitting smoking cigarettes on the pavement outside a large villa. The bloke, who is English and about the same age as myself, is wearing a shiny, grey short-sleeved dress shirt, beige shorts and canvas espadrilles. He's pasty, balding and a bit podgy. His much younger and very bored wife is dressed in skinny jeans and high heels. I'm guessing their beachwear is in the rucksack that sits between them on the pavement.

Alex jumps out to greet them and the guy instantly moans at him about his timekeeping. Alex apologises and repeats his complaints about the resort geography. Ignoring me completely, the couple clamber into the back of the minibus and continue smoking in silence.

Eventually, we find the main road leading out of the resort. Alex has his foot flat to the floor to make up lost time, although the minibus struggles northwards, asthmatically. As we drive I ask him about himself, but he gives very little away. He does reveal he's lived in Fuerteventura for a couple of years and tells me that the surfing, particularly in the winter, is "epic".

I earnestly share my reasons for wanting to learn to surf and tell him how my personal journey has led me to this day, but he's got his face pushed to the windscreen and I think he looks remarkably tense for someone who spends much of his time in the ocean.

Forty minutes later and we arrive in the town of Corralejo on the north-eastern coast of the island. It's much busier and bigger than the area I've been staying in and filled with tourist shops. According to Alex, this is where a lot of the locals live.

Even though he says he lives here too, we spend another hour driving around the narrow streets looking for more surf school students.

By now it's getting on for 1pm and I'm sort of wondering when I'll actually see a beach.

I'm still working hard at appearing relaxed though, and fill Alex in on my nautical family history as he crunches through the gears and negotiates the heavy Corralejo traffic.

"I think I have the sea in my blood," I tell him. "I just have this need to tap into all that energy, you know?"

"Yeah. Sea in your blood. Yeah. Brilliant."

I think he'll maybe understand better than most about what's driven me to learn to surf, but I'm coming to the conclusion he's probably heard this kind of guff every day for the past two years. I'm also suddenly conscious of sounding like an extra from the film *Point Break* and decide to shut up about 'The Journey' from now on.

Following smooth, wide roads that cut across Fuerteventura's Martian-like landscape, we make a brief stop in the village of Lajares, where Alex loads up on water and pastries from a little bakery. Another 10 minutes of driving and we roll into El Cotillo, a fishing village on the north-western tip of the island. It looks like a set from a spaghetti western, with white stone buildings and a lot of dust blowing around.

We take a left up a side street and the road becomes a dirt track crossing a flat, desert-like expanse of coastline overlooked by dormant volcanoes. I can see vehicles parked along the edge of the cliffs. Several have surfboards stacked on top. Crucially, I can see the ocean. This has to be our final destination.

Turning off the main track we head south towards the cliff top parking area, bumping across rocks and throwing up clouds of dust. We park next to a battered white Toyota pickup truck that has a stack of brightly coloured surfboards piled in the back.

The door of the pickup opens and out steps a small and jovial Dutch guy called Bram who's brought two more students for Alex, both English girls in their early 20s. There are others who've made their own way to the beach, so our group's now 10-strong.

Alex and Bram start untying the ropes holding the boards in place while the rest of us stand around taking in the scene and feeling a bit useless. Below our vantage point is a huge beach curving north towards the small harbour of El Cotillo. To the south the beach hugs a broken coastline of steep, flat-topped cliffs.

The water beneath us is an intense blue, but the wind is whipping up white horses across its surface. There are tattered yellow lifeguard flags flying from poles on the beach, though I have no idea yet what these mean.

A smiling Bram lifts a large blue plastic drum full of wetsuits out of the back of the pickup. Instantly measuring each of us by eye, he distributes the suits. I get the only extra large one – a black and white short-sleeved affair that's seen better days.

And then it's finally time to get my hands on a surfboard. Bram and Alex invite everyone to take one from the back of the truck. The boards are long, thick and spongy. I don't know it yet, but these are soft-topped foam beginner boards, or 'foamies'. Their length and volume makes paddling easier and their forgiving spongy construction supposedly ensures the safety of other water users.

The boards are mostly yellow and blue, though there are a couple of slightly longer orange versions. Alex suggests I take one of these as, apparently, it'll be better suited to my height and weight. The board, which has a thin coating of surfboard wax for traction, sports a number of holes as if it's been stored with a family of mice. But it's still a surfboard and I'm delighted to be finally clutching one.

Boards under our arms, we follow Alex down a steep, dusty path to the beach. The sand is burning hot and those of us who have removed our flip-flops quickly put them back on again. Alex trots across it barefoot, unaffected by the temperature.

The messy waves, loudly impacting along the shoreline, seem much larger now we're down on the sand and I feel the first surge of apprehension rising in my stomach. We self-consciously pull on our wetsuits, laughing, struggling and sweating with the effort and unfamiliarity of it all. This is my first time in a wetsuit and I can't believe how restrictive and hot it is. I also think it makes me look fat.

The training starts off well enough. Although we're all boiling hot in our suits, we do a short warm-up, jogging back and forth along the beach a few times. Alex then tells us to form a circle around him and we follow his lead with a series of exercises, rotating our arms and stretching our legs.

And then it's down to the real business of the day. Lying prone on our boards, Alex demonstrates how to paddle and "pop-up" into a surfer stance. This is the standard instructional stuff I hoped I'd get and, thankfully, I find it fairly straightforward.

I also know from my prior research that I'm classed as a regular footer, standing on the board with my left foot forward and my right foot close to the tail. The other way around and I'd be known as a 'goofy' footer.

Alex walks around the circle of students, checking our technique and advising on foot placement. He reaches a German girl who seems to be having a few problems in deciding what foot to have near the front of the board.

"Regular or goofy?" he asks her. The girl looks puzzled. "Are you regular or goofy?" he asks again, slightly irritated.

"I . . . I . . . I don't understand," she blurts out, looking as if she's going to cry. Alex sighs, steps on a board and illustrates the difference in surfboard stances. I'm taken aback at his flash of impatience, given he's never actually explained any of this to the group.

"Regular, like this," he says, left foot forward on the board, "goofy, like this," switching legs.

"I don't know!" shouts the now tearful German girl, looking baffled. Alex walks off leaving her frowning and red-faced. She avoids my encouraging smile and looks ready to go home.

"Ok," shouts Alex. "Wade out with your boards at your sides, turn around and try and belly board in on the white water. Then you can try popping up."

With that he wanders back to the shade of a large rock and sits down to observe from behind his sunglasses.

I'd expected the training element of the course to be longer than this, but instead I'm wading out into what looks to be a pretty heavy shore break with my huge orange board at my side. I'm excited and scared, but it's finally time to call my own bluff. I wanted to learn to surf and here I am.

I feel the water starting to lift me off my feet and decide this might be a good place to stop. I'm also conscious of a strong current running south along the shoreline. It pushes against my thighs, trying to unbalance me. Further offshore, a wave starts to crumble into a soupy mass of white water. Heart racing, I awkwardly turn my board around so the nose is facing the beach and clamber on. The rest of the class, spread out in a line like troops wading ashore on D-Day, is trying to do the same thing.

I hear the wave approach with a loud hissing noise and my heart rate rockets. I'm still trying to look behind me as the oncoming wave decimates our ranks. Some of the class haven't yet completed their turns – others have made it to the prone position and are paddling furiously but going nowhere. Boards flip into the air and bodies disappear in the white water.

I'm also engulfed and the next few seconds are completely disorientating. Eyes tightly shut and body tensed, I'm rolled along the seabed with an unexpected ferocity. Feeling my legs hit the sandy bottom I stand up in the shallows, water streaming out of my nose. I'm breathing hard and my heart is still hammering, but I'm also smiling. I realise this is my first official surf wipeout, even though there was no actual surfing going on.

I wade back out into the ocean with renewed confidence, pushing my board over the oncoming white water. Although there are people all around me, I'm conscious only of the sounds and smells of the sea. The warm wind is blowing spray into my face and I can taste salt. The green water is clear and I can see the sandbank below my feet.

This time I push my board a little further out, beyond my line of classmates. I can no longer feel the bottom and lie sideways across the board, taking in the scene. A metaphorical wave of satisfaction washes across me as I contemplate where I am and what I'm doing.

The sense of calm doesn't last long. A much larger wave rears up ahead of me and for a second I'm transfixed by the process in which it turns from a silent and smooth green and blue mass, to a hissing and spitting avalanche of white water. I pedal my legs frantically to get onto my board and turn it around to face the beach, but I'm scooped up before I make it fully on. The impact is more brutal this time and again I'm rolled along the seabed, staying underwater for a few seconds longer.

But I surface unshaken and head back out, determined to stay on my board for the next wave. It comes and I'm swamped again, a process that's repeated for the next 30 minutes.

I'm starting to get tired, as are some of my classmates. A few of them are managing to ride the white water prone on their boards, but three of the girls have given up and are sitting on the beach, drinking water and talking to Alex. He's not paying much attention to the rest of us. My arms are starting to ache from wrestling my board through the currents and white water and there's a growing sense that actually riding a wave is going to be much, much harder than I'd thought.

Just about ready to give up, I finally manage to ride to the beach prone on my stomach and the sensation is mind-blowing. My board seems to come to life, rocketing towards shore with no visible means of propulsion and for a brief moment I get some idea of what it must be like to surf properly. Suddenly re-energised, I head straight back out with the intention of trying to stand up on the next wave, but every single attempt fails.

I briefly make it to one knee, but wobble and fall off the side. Frustration starts to grow along with fatigue and I decide to take a break.

A blonde girl in a bikini, who I assume is Alex's girlfriend, has joined him. She's got her legs wrapped around his waist and he's stroking her hair. The three young women from my group are now sat further away, chatting and eating sandwiches. The German girl is sitting alone, despondently looking out to sea.

The balding guy and his wife from my resort are nowhere

to be seen, but then I spot them floundering around in the shallows, 100 metres south of our position. Alex suddenly notices them too, stands up and whistles. They look over and he signals for them to move back up the beach. Clearly he's paying more attention than I'd thought.

After reapplying sun cream and drinking the remainder of my water, I head back out to try again, but my efforts are no better than before. I wade out, turn my board around, climb on and paddle, but I simply cannot stand up. Each time I attempt to spring into a surfing stance, my toes clobber the tail of the board and I end up with my feet briefly together in completely the wrong position. Then I fall off. It's starting to irritate me hugely and I look to the beach, hopeful I'll get some pointers from Alex, but he's too busy hugging his girlfriend to notice my predicament.

My classmates have had enough for the day and soon I'm the only one left in the water. I manage to ride in on my stomach again, but my arms are killing me and I have a headache from dehydration. Alex whistles and points to his watch and I'm actually glad that it's time to go home.

Staggering back up the beach, I notice the German girl's family has arrived. She's deep in conversation with them and her father has his arm around her. He then goes over to talk to Alex. The dad, a large, bearded bloke, is waving his arms around, but I can't hear what he's saying. Alex remains silent, eyes hidden behind his huge sunglasses. The girl then stomps back off up the track with her family towards the parking area, leaving her board and wetsuit on the sand.

Wrapped up in my own surf-related problems I don't ask Alex what was going down, though I could suggest a few reasons why the girl's dad might be less than happy. Instead, I make a joke about how hard I'm finding the act of standing up. Alex suggests I might need a bigger board and promises to bring one to tomorrow's session.

Back in our resort, exhausted and a little depressed, I replayed the day's events. Whilst outwardly enthusiastic for the sake of Shona and David, things hadn't panned out the way I thought they might. I felt stiff and inept in the water and disappointed with the quality of the instruction. But it was a start and I also had that promise of a bigger board to hang my hopes on.

CHAPTER 2

Day two of my surfing course turns out to be a near repeat of day one. Alex is over an hour late picking me up, but the silent smoking couple are already onboard and we head straight back north, saying very little to each other on the journey.

We arrive in Corralejo where Alex drives up a narrow side street and stops outside a shabby white apartment building. He honks the horn and a stocky young blonde man in his 20s appears out of a doorway, screwing his eyes tightly shut against the sunlight. The guy has a rolled up towel under his arm and is clutching a plastic carrier bag in his hand.

Climbing aboard the minibus, he says "All right?" in a strong Yorkshire accent. "I'm Fred," he declares, sitting down behind me.

Fred, who is the epitome of friendliness, explains that this is day three of his two-week 'surf camp' deal with the school.

Hungover and bleary-eyed, he bursts out laughing when I ask him what he's learned so far. He loudly states that the surf school's instruction and accommodation is 'shite', but adds that he doesn't really care. He's spent the first couple of days of his camp being roasted on a beach and reveals he's not actually done much surfing yet either, which is a fairly worrying revelation. But he's enjoying the nightlife in Corralejo and has been betting on horses a lot.

I'm tired by the time we reach Cotillo and feeling less than enthusiastic about the session ahead. The sea looks rougher than it did the previous day and there are red flags flying from the poles on the beach.

Half a dozen students are waiting for us on the cliff top. I grab the black and white extra large wetsuit and go to select a board. This time there are two huge white boards lying in the back of the pickup. These are Bics, a robust budget brand of surfboard, made out of a type of plastic by the same people who produce the pens and razors. Alex picks one out of the truck and hands it to me, with some effort.

"Yeah, this is your board, man," he says with a mystic edge that appeals to me. "This is the board for you. You'll catch loads of waves on this."

Measuring over eight feet long, the board weighs as much as a small ferry. A token layer of patchy surf wax and sand covers the tired orange and black pinstripe graphics, but it looks more like a proper surfboard and therefore sets me apart from the others on their foamies. This gives my seriously deluded ego a boost and Fred's also clearly impressed by my apparent graduation to surfing's big time. I get him to take my picture with the board, marking the moment when I become something more akin to a surfer. Fred's delighted when Alex tells him to grab the other Bic.

"You guys know the drill," Alex says to us. "Just head out and do what you did yesterday."

We walk off down the beach towards the shoreline as Alex launches into his warm-up routine with the rest of the students. The smoking couple have opted to stay onshore and join in with the newcomers.

Just as we reach the water's edge a huge wave, easily over six feet high, rears up from the depths of the Atlantic. It sounds like thunder as it collapses onto the sandbank, churning up the shoreline and turning the water a light greenish-brown. Another wave of a similar size is right behind it. Fred and me back off from the surging white water and worriedly look towards Alex for guidance. His students are all watching the waves with open mouths. He trots down to where we're standing. "Um, yeah, just stay in front of that," he says, pointing to another imploding mountain of ocean. "That wave's one-and-a-half times overhead," he adds before running back to get his pupils warmed up.

Fred laughs nervously as we wade out through the shore break with our boards at our sides. I'm saying nothing, my mind conjuring up all kinds of unpleasant underwater scenarios.

The ocean has briefly settled down again, but we can feel the strong current pulling at our legs as we push on to where we think might be a safe spot to paddle from. Then the sea in front of us inflates. It's another massive wave, only this time we're right in its path. Fred turns towards me screaming, "Oh, fuck!" as he ditches his board and goes to dive under the face of the wave. I should be doing the same, but for some reason I decide to try and meet this challenge head on.

Clambering onto my huge board to a soundtrack of roaring, I start paddling furiously, but absolutely nothing happens. A split second later I jump from stasis to hyperspace. My brain can't cope with the launchpad magnitude of acceleration, but remembering my lesson from the day before, I optimistically try to stand up. Instantly, the board heads nose first for the ocean floor in an action known as pearling. It flips upside down and I'm driven face first into the sand.

It's a horrible sensation and although it only lasts a couple of seconds, I feel as if I'm watching the scene unfold from outside my body. I end up on all fours in the shallows, with sandy water pouring from my nose. My arms are incredibly sore and I have what feels like toothache in my shoulder joints. Fred, meanwhile, has surfaced a few feet away from me and is heading for dry land as if his life depends on it.

A bearded, sandal-wearing tourist in his 50s runs up and takes my picture as I try to stand up. I haven't the energy to tell him to fuck off, let alone kill him. I get up, water still dribbling out of my nose, mouth and ears, and stagger back to where Alex is instructing his students in how to pop-up. I collapse on the sand beside him.

"Jesus fucking Christ!"

"Yeah," he replies to my stream of oaths. "Now you can say that you've surfed a wave one-and-a-half times overhead!"

His comment briefly restores my pride and provides some damage repair for my ego, but then I realise that being chewed up by a wave isn't the same as surfing one.

Alex's students ignore me, locked into the pretend paddling/pop-up routine. It looks so easy on the beach. It felt easy when I did it the previous day. Now I'm suddenly scared to try it again on the water. I watch the students as they head off into the shore break, unjustifiably pissed off that a few get to their knees within minutes, making short wobbly rides to the beach. One of the girls in the class briefly makes it to her feet, getting a whistle and thumbs up from Alex.

I grab my board and head back to try again. Fred is further down the beach, flailing around in the white water. It's not long until I'm doing the same, exhaustion clouding my mind and ensuring I never get to my feet for the entire session. The sea pounds me relentlessly and I'm struggling to handle the heavy board, a fact that also annoys me.

After a couple of hours, the pain in my arms and shoulders overpowers any desire to keep trying, and I stagger back out of the water to collapse on the hot sand, utterly exhausted. I strip off my wetsuit and let the sun warm my aching joints. I'm done. Thankfully, it's not long until Alex calls the session to an end.

After loading the boards into the pickup, we climb wearily into the van. I remind Alex that I've not yet paid the 30 euro balance for my course – Shona's already paid 60 euros by credit card, with the school advising her that I should pay the remainder 'at the beach' – and I hand him a 50 euro note. He sticks it in his wallet and gives me a 20 in change. I'm slightly concerned that he's not noted this payment down on any official document, but I tell myself to stop being so uptight about administration on a surfing course.

CHAPTER 3

The final day of my course arrives. I almost call the surf school to cancel because the pain in my joints is so bad. But I feel determined to come away from this course with something other than sunburn and aching muscles.

I walk down through the resort to await my lift. The van, now being driven by the eternally cheerful Bram, arrives almost on time. He chatters about the injuries he's sustained on the reefs around Fuerteventura and assures me surfing is the hardest of all board sports to learn.

We head straight for Corralejo where we collect two young Irish guys, Sean and Pete, who have signed up for a day's course. Then we stop outside Fred's accommodation. He appears at the door dressed in spectacularly lurid gold and white board shorts and a tight black rash vest. This ensemble provides a stark contrast to the raging pink sunburn on his face, arms and legs. I say something about his professional-looking gear and he explains there's been a sale on at some surf shop in town.

The pickup truck and its load of boards are waiting for us when we arrive at the beach. Standing beside it, arms folded across his chest, is a dark, muscular and stern-looking guy in faded orange board shorts. Bram introduces him to us as Carlos, a Portuguese surf instructor who works with the school.

Carlos starts handing out wetsuits from the back of the pickup, thrusting a pink and black Medium into my arms. I think he's joking, but his dour expression is set like granite. He doesn't speak much English and I don't speak any Portuguese. He looks puzzled as I babble about my need for an extra large, so I take the initiative and root around in the plastic drum until I find the black and white suit I've come to call my own.

As Bram hands out boards from the back of the truck, Carlos pulls a sheet of paper and a pen off the dashboard. Studying it closely, he moves along the line of students, ticking off names and nodding. When he gets to me I show him my name on the sheet. I notice there are 'PAID' ticks for days one and two next to my name, but a question mark next to day three. Carlos stabs a massive finger at the question mark.

"Pay," he says, as if he was professionally collecting a debt and would shortly be helping himself to my watch and camera.

"I have," I answer. "I gave Alex the last 30 euros yesterday." Carlos looks suspicious, but shrugs and sticks the sheet of paper back into the truck.

The final day of the course is a tragi-comedy, acted out through a fog of frustration and fatigue. Alex spends 90 percent of his time talking to his girlfriend on the beach and stroking her hair. The only time he pays any attention to what's going off in the water is when someone gets carried too far south on the current. Then he leaps to his feet, runs to the water's edge and whistles while waving his arms in a northerly direction. Carlos, meanwhile, enjoys a private surf session on one of the school's foam boards.

Students stagger out of the water and retire to the beach, exhausted and dejected, enviously watching the people who've signed up with what seems to be a more professional surf school operating nearby. Aside from their pristine, logo-emblazoned van, these students are getting loads of attention from an enthusiastic instructor who runs up and down the beach, whooping at every hint of progress from his charges. I notice Alex watching them.

Once our class are all out of the water, Alex grabs one of the battered orange foam boards and trots off into the sea to join Carlos. He clears the shore break with ease and paddles at speed out to where his colleague is waiting for another set, or group of waves, to arrive. Then they're both up and riding. Theirs is an impressive display and serves to remind us all how crap we are. They stay out at sea for another 30 minutes.

"Just look at him," says one of the Irish guys, pointing out to where Carlos is tearing across the face of a small foamy wave. "What a fecking poseur. Do you think there are sharks out there? I fecking hope so."

Eventually, Carlos and Alex paddle back to shore. The session kind of fizzles out and I want to ask when I'll be learning about wave selection, tides and all that ocean knowledge stuff promised in the course blurb. Instead, we climb back up the boiling sand dunes to the van and load the boards into the pickup.

We're just about ready to head off when a little silver hire car skids to a halt beside us. Inside are the smoking couple from my resort. The bloke jumps out and accosts Alex who's tightening the straps holding our boards in place.

"Where the fuck were you this morning?" the smoking guy asks, clearly incandescent.

"Um, sorry man. What?" Alex looks baffled.

"You were supposed to pick us up this morning!"

"Who are you?"

"We signed up for a fucking three day course! You've fucking picked us up the past two fucking days!"

"Um. Yeah, right. Um. Let me just check." Alex leans inside the van and retrieves some torn paperwork that's stuffed down the side of the driver's seat. He looks shell-shocked and is repeatedly saying "shit" under his breath. One of the Irish guys is trying not to laugh.

Alex steps out and checks the sheet, reading it with an intensity that suggests he might be losing his sight. He's still none the wiser as to who this couple are. The bloke is pumped up for a fight, dancing back and forth on the balls of his feet. His wife stays in the car, smoking and looking bored.

"You lot are fucking useless!" shouts the guy, shocking Alex into a sudden realisation as to who they are.

Alex makes a grovelling apology, blaming the mix-up on the admin person back at surf school headquarters. A study in passive body language, he places his left hand on his chest and bows slightly, but the soulful right-on gesture doesn't work for angry bloke who looks like he's going to rip Alex's head off. The guy stomps off back to his hire car and roars away in a cloud of sand and dust.

Alex, face red, says little during the return journey to Corralejo. He briefly flashes with irritation when the Irish guys in the back of the van start waving at a following police car.

"Don't fuck with the cops here!" pleads Alex. "They've already pulled me over, like, four times this month!"

The Irish lads and Fred are dropped in the centre of Corralejo and we say our goodbyes. I wish Fred luck for the remainder of his course, genuinely hoping he'll emerge as a competent surfer after his fortnight. But I don't hold out much hope for him or anyone else who signs up with this outfit.

Alex takes me back to the resort in silence. Fighting the urge to fall asleep against the van window, all I'm thinking about is getting into our apartment and swallowing a load of water and painkillers. My arms are killing me and my head is aching. Alex drops me off, says I need to let them know how my surfing goes – "Send us pictures" – and then he's gone.

Although the pain in my body faded as our family holiday progressed, I couldn't shake off the sense of failure and disappointment I felt at never having caught a wave during my course. Outwardly I blamed the quality of instruction and the boards I'd been given to use, but deep down I knew I wasn't fit enough, or sufficiently flexible to surf. Granted, better instruction might have helped, but I wondered if subconsciously I was still too scared to commit to forcing myself to stand up on a wave.

The day we returned home to Scotland, I found the surf school had charged 30 euros to Shona's credit card. I mailed them asking why and received a terse reply about how I'd left on the last day of the course without settling the balance. I mailed back explaining how I'd given Alex a 50 euro note and asked them to refund the card charge. Instead, they told me Alex had no recollection of being paid.

It was the final straw. Raging at their implication I was a liar, I told them what I thought of their operation and reluctantly played the journalist card, threatening to write an article revealing how hopeless they were. The money was paid back the same day and I brooded for the rest of the week, feeling like I'd been forced into becoming The Man.

CHAPTER 4

The surf course in Fuerteventura hadn't delivered the marine epiphany I'd been seeking. The rather casual approach to teaching and the subsequent fight about the money had left a bad taste in my mouth. And my joints still ached from the three days I'd spent floundering around in the Cotillo beach break.

Keen that Shona didn't feel as if she'd completely wasted her money, I enthused about the course to her – and anyone else who asked how it had gone. One of the lifeguards at our local swimming pool was a surfer so I gave him an edited rundown of my adventure, hopeful I'd get an invite to come and join him and the handful of guys who I knew tackled the plentiful waves around Orkney's coasts. He didn't suggest it. In hindsight, that was probably a sensible decision on his part, but his slight indifference to my cause stung a little.

As outwardly upbeat as I was about Fuerteventura, the course had been a wake-up call. Surfing was much harder than I thought it would be.

With no board of my own and no invite forthcoming to try anyone else's, I felt like a rudderless, dry-docked ship. I could have bought a second hand board and wetsuit and just headed out to a local beach, but the seas around Orkney genuinely scared me. Tackling them solo wasn't an option. Even if I'd had the guts required, I wouldn't have known where and when to go.

Instead, I trawled the internet searching for Scottish surf schools, hoping I could secure some professional help. I quickly found one based in Thurso, on Scotland's northern coast. I'd passed through the town thousands of times over the years – the ferry to Orkney sailed from there – but I'd only recently come to learn about its world class reef break, named Thurso East. I reasoned that a surf school based near an apparently legendary wave – one frequently used as a backdrop for professional contests – must be good, though I also hoped that riding it wouldn't be a course requirement.

A guy called Andy Bain ran the school. His website, which included pictures of him surfing enormous Thurso East waves, looked professional. I picked up the phone and told him all about Fuerteventura and how I desperately needed to learn how to surf, properly. Laid back and affable, he listened patiently to my blabbering and agreed to call me when it looked like there might be a hint of swell at Dunnet Bay, the beach to the east of Thurso he used for lessons. While awaiting his call, I pitched the idea of an article on learning to surf to the editor of a Scottish national newspaper's weekend magazine. They'd been publishing some of my outdoors articles and when I explained how I was heading to the wild Caithness coast to learn to surf after a failed attempt in the Canaries, they were sold.

With a commission in the bag, I contacted my colleague Stan, a photographer I occasionally collaborated with on feature work. He sounded enthusiastic about the job and assured me he'd get hold of an underwater camera to take some good action shots for the magazine.

Weeks passed with no call from Andy. I was starting to think I was about to become the victim of another surf school admin error, but in late August he rang with good news. There was a small swell on the way and it looked as if it might produce a modest wave on the beach at Dunnet.

I arrange to meet Stan the next day and we catch the small passenger ferry that runs between Orkney and John o' Groats on the Scottish mainland during the summer months. Andy has said he'll pick us up from there in his van and take us to the beach.

It's a glorious day and the sea is flat calm during our 45-minute ferry crossing. So calm in fact that Stan's not convinced there'll be any surfing done. Regardless, he's brought some enormous lenses with him for shooting pictures from the beach, plus a large military kitbag, the contents of which remain a mystery.

Disembarking at John o' Groats, I instantly spot Andy standing amongst the throngs of tourists buying cheap tartan souvenirs from shops near the pier. A huge, longhaired bear of a guy, he's dressed in board shorts and dark sunglasses. He greets Stan and me and leads us to his van for the short drive to Dunnet Bay. His transport is in better condition than the van in Fuerteventura and I take that as a good omen.

Andy, a native of Thurso, tells me he trained as a chef after leaving school, but it's been a surfer's path he's followed since.

"I had to have some type of trade so I could work in the

summer and then go away for the winter and surf for a few months, just generally following the weather and the waves," he says as we drive along the Caithness coast towards Dunnet. His quest took him around some of the planet's best-known surfing spots, but he kept coming home to Caithness and the break at Thurso East. As I'll later learn, he first began surfing this unforgiving wave wearing shorts and a set of goalkeeper gloves. Now he's regarded as the main man in the water there, policing the break and keeping the increasing crowds of surfers in line, in between riding monster waves.

I know none of this of course and drone on about my bad experience in Fuerteventura, only occasionally remembering I'm supposed to be interviewing Andy for the magazine.

I've signed up for a two-hour session and Andy's certain I'll get up on my feet before the time's up. My confidence wrecked by the Cotillo experience, I'm not totally convinced.

We arrive at Dunnet and park next to a public toilet block. Walking up to the top of the grassy sand dunes, the full expanse of this magnificent horseshoe bay is revealed.

Andy starts explaining the mechanics of what's happening at sea, pointing out our prospective surfing spot in the middle of the bay. Although his briefing can't help me a huge amount at this stage, it's the kind of oceanic insight I've been craving. However, I can tell that the waves look pretty benign, which suits me just fine.

"I always use Dunnet as it's a great beach for learning," says Andy as we walk back to the van. "We get a lot of people from places where the surf isn't as consistent. They might have had a lesson on holiday down in Cornwall, or the Canaries, and they've come back and want to try and continue that learning process."

· I clearly fall into this category. I feel a rush of apprehension as Andy opens the back of his van and selects a wetsuit for me. We get suited up in the beach car park, grab a couple of huge yellow foam boards, and a flagpole, and walk down a wooden boardwalk that cuts through the sand dunes to the beach. Stan wanders off to the base of a dune, dumps his kitbag and starts fiddling with cameras and lenses.

I head down towards the water's edge with Andy who plants the flagpole on the beach, unfurling a British Surfing Association pennant for use as a safety marker. He then tells me to dig a hole for my board's fins so we can practice popping up. The contrast between his teaching style and what I experienced in Fuerteventura is already noticeable.

My previous instruction had me leap from a prone paddling position, straight into the classic crouched surfer pose. Clearly, I never fully mastered that and was expecting to go through the same process with Andy. Instead, he breaks the journey from paddling to standing into distinctive segments.

"Bring your right knee up until it's under your chest and put your weight on your arms," he explains. "Then bring your left leg around and place your foot in the centre of the board. Now stand up, keeping your knees bent and your weight over your front foot."

We do this drill a few times while Stan takes some shots, and then it's out into the waves to try it for real. Stan shoots a couple of pictures of Andy and me walking along the beach towards the shoreline, before running back up to the dunes to fit a massive telephoto lens to his camera.

Clutching my huge yellow foam board under my arm I wade out into the bay with Andy at my side. The sun's warm and the wind light. It feels good to be back in the sea again. The swell's smaller than it was at Cotillo and the beach is altogether gentler.

Once I start to feel the swell lift me off my feet, I clamber onto the board in a fairly undignified manner and lie facing the beach. Andy, who's taller than me, stands alongside and says he's going to push me into a few waves to get me started.

A small swell arrives and Andy shoves the tail of my board. I take a couple of strokes and try to remember my drill from the beach, but my brain reverts to what it learned in Fuerteventura and I rush the whole thing, trying to leap up in one go. The result is the first of several dunkings.

Andy patiently goes over the beach drills again and again. I relax and gradually it all starts to hit home.

And then it happens. I paddle into a wave, methodically following Andy's earlier instructions and suddenly I'm on my feet. My brain's circuitry is jammed with unfamiliar sensations. I feel about 50ft tall, looking down at my board as if through someone else's eyes. I gingerly push my left foot forward on the front of my craft, creating a sensation akin to pressing the opposite poles of two magnets together. The board's alive. I'm connected to the ocean's energy, yet somehow floating above it. Endorphins are rushing through my body and I feel an overwhelming sense of euphoria.

Although the ride only lasts a few seconds, I feel as if I'm up there for hours. I raise my arms in joyous triumph and start shouting. I can't help myself. Then I fall off into the shallows, fighting back tears. Stan's smiling, Andy's smiling and I'm still shouting.

Stan tells me he's going to get changed for the water shots and jogs over to his kitbag under the dunes. I paddle back out to Andy, talking non-stop about how great the ride felt. Although he's probably seen this reaction a thousand times, Andy seems genuinely happy for me. I keep thanking him for what he's shown me and I want to try again.

Onshore, Stan is pulling something black out of his kitbag and I assume he's brought a wetsuit for the water shots. I ride another wave into the beach, feeling as if I've exploded through some seemingly impenetrable mental barrier and entered another realm.

Standing in the shallows, beaming, I watch Stan walk awkwardly down the beach towards me dressed in an enormous baggy black dry suit he says he's borrowed from a mate. It's ancient and peppered with odd-looking outlets for valves. It looks like something you'd wear to storm an embassy, or go into space with. Clearly way too big for him, he assures me it'll "do the job."

Stan then reveals that his other specialised equipment for this ocean assignment is a £4.99 blue and yellow plastic 'waterproof' camera. Apparently, earlier in the week, he'd tried to scrounge a professional underwater camera housing from a sceptical contact in the commercial dive world, but failed.

We wade out to sea for the action photo shoot segment of the job. Stan, who's a good bit shorter than I am, soon has to start swimming. He does a kind of breaststroke variation where all his limbs are in motion at once, except he's not actually moving anywhere. It's like watching a frog in a bucket of glue. I'm standing on the sandy bottom, water up to my thighs, holding my yellow foam board by my side, but Stan's doing his swimming thing around my knees, clutching the cheapo waterproof camera and blowing out hard with a surprised expression on his face.

Stan wants me to lie on the board so he can try a shot with a wave breaking over my head. He positions himself right at the nose of the board and sticks the tiny camera on top of it. I try to tell him that the tip of the board is now pointed straight at his throat, but I'm too late. I feel the tail being picked up, white water thunders over my head and I see Stan's eyes widen before he disappears beneath me.

He resurfaces a few seconds later, spitting out water and trying to advance the film with the camera's little plastic winder. We try for this shot again and again, and each time Stan narrowly misses having his throat crushed by the board and my flailing body. Eventually he gives up and waddles back to shore to shoot from the beach with his professional dry land equipment.

I join Andy again and try for a few more waves, but I'm emotionally and physically spent and my two hours are almost up. After we head back in Stan takes a few pictures of Andy, stripped to the waist and posing Hawaiian style, with his board propped vertically against his back.

On the way back to the van I can't stop talking about the sensations I felt out on the water. Stan says something about my waves not being very big, but Andy jumps to my defence. "Naw man, he did all right," he drawls. He then gives me a 'surfer shake', as if he's about to arm-wrestle me. I almost burst with joy.

Waiting for the ferry back home from Caithness after my lesson, I felt like a different person. While Stan wandered around taking pictures of the scenery at John o' Groats, I sat in the late summer sun contemplating the day and trying to hold onto the feeling I'd got on that first wave. Yes, the swell had been tiny and my wobbly rides brief, but I'd crossed a huge mental barrier.

Memories of Fuerteventura had evaporated the moment I'd stood up and glided across the ocean. The sensation exceeded all my expectations. I'd heard the expression 'only a surfer knows the feeling' and thought it was probably cheesy, bumper sticker philosophy. But now, with a couple of short, tentative rides to my name, I kind of understood. I had, in a further example of hokey surfing parlance, 'gone to see the surf wizard' and there was no going back.

As soon as I walked in the door at home, Shona and David knew I'd caught a wave. If I'd joined a religious cult or found enlightenment, I suspect my expression would have been exactly the same.

CHAPTER 5

My next problem was how to keep the momentum going. Aside from the fact I had no surfboard, the Orkney weather was starting to become more autumnal and unpredictable. On walks around the west coast of the islands I could see the Atlantic swells building and even if I'd had something to ride, I was wary of launching off any local beaches. I still held out hope for an invite from one of the local surf crew, but I didn't know any of them well enough to ask for guidance and they probably viewed me as a complete liability.

Landlocked and frustrated, I called Andy a couple of times to discuss the possibility of my coming back over for more lessons, but he was clearly of the opinion that I should just buy a board, find a beach and get on with it. I checked out boards online, but had little idea of what I needed and I also lacked a wetsuit. On a freelance income, it was hard to justify buying a board or a suit, but I vaguely thought I might pick up something second hand.

With the arrival of winter I resigned myself to the fact I probably wouldn't be surfing again until the following year. Huge waves, no equipment and zero contact with any of the local surfers made it a total non-starter.

On Christmas Day, however, I was stunned when Shona presented me with a wetsuit, and then an enormous bubble-wrapped package that was clearly a surfboard. And not just any surfboard, but a custom-made mini-mal (basically a cut down longboard, or mal, with plenty of volume for easy paddling and stability).

Unknown to me, Shona had called Andy not long after my successful lesson and asked him what kind of board I'd need. He'd then contacted a surfboard shaper he knew and given him a rundown of my size, weight and ability. The result was a 7'10" long board, thick enough to support my 220lb bulk. The wooden stringer – the thin strip of wood running the length of a surfboard – had 'For Dave' pencilled onto it by the shaper, Simon Noble.

I welled up when I unwrapped it, puzzling David who thought I should be running around the room, ecstatic. But he quickly realised these were tears of joy.

Never having handled a custom surfboard before, I was almost too scared to touch it. It was large, but felt light in comparison to the industrial strength Bic I'd tried to ride in Fuerteventura. Pure white, it had a luminescent quality to it and I ran my hands lightly across its surface, as if it were made of rice paper. It reeked of polyurethane resin and fibreglass, but the pungent smell was all part of the unfamiliar, hugely exciting package. My own custom surfboard. I couldn't believe it.

As soon as Christmas was out of the way, I went online to buy a travel bag for the board. I also bought an 8ft long leash and several blocks of Sex Wax surfboard wax. I had no idea how to apply this stuff and watched a video on YouTube before tentatively waxing up the board in my garage. I had to watch another instructional film in order to learn how to attach the leash.

Having nowhere to store something so large, I built a rack to hang from the garage ceiling and wrapped the whole thing in foam plumbing insulation and bubble-wrap.

The reverence and care I attached to every task associated with my new board was close to neurotic, but I had a very strong sense of its significance as key to an exciting new chapter in my life. T-shirts and flip-flops were one thing, but a custom board was the real deal.

When all the preparatory work surrounding my new possession was done though, I was faced with the realisation that I'd actually have to step up and take the board into the ocean at some stage – most likely alone.

I frequently found myself taking the board down from its rack and just looking at it. It had already taken on a personality – quiet, brooding and primed for action – but I wasn't sure if I was up to the task of breaking it in solo.

Finally, in mid January, I take it down from its rack, strap it to the car and head out to the east of the island where I think the sea might be more manageable. I arrive at a beach where I normally walk the dog and, whilst it's very windy, the waves are small.

Pulling on my brand new wetsuit, boots and gloves, I feel as if I'm kitting myself out in armour before facing certain death on the battlefield. I become acutely aware of my heavy breathing and hammering heartbeat. I then make the classic kook (an inexperienced surfer) error of attaching my leg leash before I'm anywhere near the sea. This means I trip over it several times as I negotiate the sand dunes and shoreline stones on my way to the water's edge.

Doing this alone feels enormously foolhardy, but I force myself not to overthink the situation and purposely wade out into the freezing North Sea like a bloody-minded Edwardian missionary entering a hostile tribal village. I look down to witness my board's christening, mentally storing the moment as another milestone in my surfing life.

A couple of choppy waves rise up and smack me in the face, denting my confidence a little, but I haul myself onto my board and start paddling around in circles. The board moves well, though it takes me a few minutes to find the optimum body position for making any kind of notable progress. I stop and try to sit up on the board as I'd seen Andy and the instructors in Fuerteventura do. Instantly I fall off. I try again repeatedly, but topple into the sea every time. The water's so cold it makes my teeth hurt.

Looking up, I'm startled to find I'm much, much further offshore than I want to be. My car, parked above the dunes, is receding and I now have a view of the whole bay. Fearing I'm about to be swept into the North Sea, I start paddling hard for shore, eventually arriving back at the safety of the beach exhausted and shaken, but satisfied I've christened my board. It wasn't surfing, but it was progress of a sort.

Weeks then passed without the board getting wet again. The winter weather, combined with my complete lack of knowledge of where and when to surf, stopped me in my tracks. I did drive to the east coast several times, but turned for home on seeing the conditions offshore, memories of being swept out into the middle of the bay still fresh in my mind.

Spring brought an improvement in the weather and I decided to take the board for a paddle around a completely flat inlet in the east of the islands, just to try and stay in contact with the ocean. Tourists and dog walkers on the shore looked at me as if I was insane.

Summer came along, and then autumn, but my board remained unused in my garage. I knew the islands' main surf spots would be lighting up as the Atlantic swells became more powerful, but I resigned myself to waiting until the following spring to tentatively try again out east, or hassle Andy for another surfing lesson in Caithness.

Fundamentally, I was too scared to bite the bullet and just go surfing properly. Paddling around flat bays, or faffing around in small, choppy shore breaks wasn't surfing and I knew it.

I was overcomplicating the whole endeavour, as I'd done with most things in my life. It was a quality I disliked in myself but found hard to change. Planning and preparation were essential factors in aviation and, I felt, sensible elements of the other outdoors activities I enjoyed. In the past – when single and childless – I'd pushed the envelope and lived, but those dramas had been played out in the familiar territory of the hills, or the sky. With surfing I was operating without any framework, beyond the lesson at Dunnet and my three days of thrashing around in Cotillo. I knew obsessive worrying really didn't fit the surfing profile, but I couldn't shake off my concerns about the potential consequences for my family of my going solo at sea. I wanted to surf, yet was stuck in a kind of phoney war with the ocean.

Standing inspecting the fresh coat of wax of my board in the garage one December evening, I had no idea I was about to get the kick up the backside I needed to change my outlook, on not just surfing, but life in general.

CHAPTER 6

I've never actually stood on my board for more than a millisecond and can't even sit upright without tipping off ungraciously, moments later. Yet here I am paddling across a thin veneer of ocean that barely conceals a minefield of enormous boulders. Fast moving walls of white-water are heading in my direction and every few seconds the bottom of my previously pristine custom surfboard grates against something sharp and geological. This is nuts and I'm terrified, wondering how on earth I was talked into this lunacy.

A few weeks earlier I'd seen a small, rusty red car driving around town with a large surfboard bag strapped to the roof. The bag was roughly the same dimensions as my own, suggesting its owner was a kindred spirit.

I subsequently saw this mystery surfer – a tanned, fit-looking bloke with close-cropped dark hair and glasses – in the supermarket. Reassuringly, his trolley was filled with fruit, vegetables and wholemeal pasta. Thinking he could be some kind of clean living 30-something surf guru, I wanted to approach him, but equally didn't want to appear like a stalker. I also worried about talking up my own surfing experience, lest I found myself invited out by this guy to catch a wave on a 20ft winter's day.

Not long after the sighting in the vegetable aisle, I picked up a severe chest infection, thanks to spending too many late nights working on magazine deadlines. Visiting the local health centre for treatment, I saw the same surfboard-topped red hatchback in the car park. I half hoped Supermarket Surf Guru was ill too, or nursing a wipeout related injury. Perhaps we could sit and shoot the breeze about waves while waiting to see a doctor.

As it turned out, he was the doctor. Embarrassed by my poor state of health, I never mentioned surfing to him. Instead, he listened to my wheezing chest and gave me an ECG, just to make sure my incessant coughing wasn't the onset of a heart attack. I wasn't sure if he'd noticed the Surfer's Path t-shirt I was wearing underneath my surf brand hoody. Clutching a prescription for antibiotics, I shuffled out of the surgery in my skate trainers, our shared passion for surfing unmentioned.

But one December evening Surf Doc turned up at our local climbing wall while I was struggling up a few routes. As well as being an accomplished surfer – as far as I knew – it turned out Doc was also an experienced climber. After he'd raced up and down the wall like a spider, I overheard him talking to a couple of climbers about surfing at the Bay of Skaill, on Orkney's west coast.

Skaill. It was the islands' main surfing spot, overlooked by the 5,000-year-old Neolithic village of Skara Brae. It was a beautiful, horseshoe bay, mobbed by busloads of tourists in the summer, but wide open to the powerful westerly swells that rolled in all winter. The waves on the bay's southerly and northerly point breaks – a point break is a place where waves form against a section of coastline jutting out into the sea – were frequently enormous and I'd watched them often, certain I'd never have enough guts or skill to get out there.

I understood that the southerly side of the bay was particularly popular with local surfers as it produced a fast moving 'left hand' wave that peeled at speed across a boulder reef (wave direction is always viewed from the perspective of the surfer and what way they have to turn to ride along the wave face). On big days the oncoming westerly swell would explode up, and occasionally over, the high headland above the surf break. Millions of gallons of white water continually thundered through a massive blowhole that had been carved through the sandstone cliffs by the relentless pounding of the Atlantic. It was a dramatic spot in a land not short on breathtaking scenery.

What terrified me most from a prospective surfer's perspective were the huge waves that would often appear further out to sea and then steam across much of the bay.

From the safety of the beach I'd watched the tiny figures of surfers sitting off the point suddenly paddling frantically to avoid these giant 'sneaker' sets. Sometimes they'd squeak over the behemoths, but at other times they'd vanish under collapsing mountains of ocean, surfacing far from where they'd been hit. But then they'd paddle back out and do it all again. It was the spectacle of the Portuguese body boarders, scaled up by a factor of 10.

The Bay of Skaill represented both the apex of my surfing aspirations and the manifestation of all my darkest fears about the ocean. To be out amongst the waves off that forbidding headland was something I sort of thought I longed for, but in all honesty I wasn't sure I'd ever be ready to deal with those conditions. It was self-indulgence to think I might be capable one day, but making the transition from inexperienced and hopeless paddler to someone who could survive out there was akin to the difference between rewiring a plug and trying to defuse a nuclear bomb. I had neither the guts nor the required knowledge for the task.

But such was my desperation to find some kind of reliable guide to help me progress my surfing ambitions, I plucked up the courage to interrupt Surf Doc between climbs, telling him I was also a surfer. He enthusiastically introduced himself as Mark. Very soon we were swapping mobile phone numbers and agreeing to meet up. Although he downplayed his experience a little, he came across as a confident guy and I was certain I'd be in safe hands as I learned the wave-riding ropes properly. Crucially, it seemed as if I was finally on the cusp of being accepted into the local surfing scene.

Two days after our climbing club exchange I'm caught off guard when Mark calls and suggests we meet up at Skaill. I tell him I've never surfed there before, but he breezily reassures me "It'll be fine."

It's a cold, clear and windy December day and I feel sick with a mixture of fear and excitement as I load my board onto the roof of the car, pack my wetsuit, gloves and boots and head west from my home in Kirkwall. When I arrive at the Bay of Skaill, Mark's already there with his girlfriend Jen, also a doctor. She's got a bodyboard and fins with her. I'm hyper-nervous, but decide to man up and just go with the flow for the day.

From the car park I can see waves breaking off the point

on the south side of the bay, but reckon we'll probably be heading to the beach for a mellow session on the shore break. It looks more than sufficient for my purposes.

But Mark has other ideas. He grabs his board and trots off down the path leading to the village of Skara Brae, overlooking the southerly point. I follow him and Jen along the edge of the farmland beyond the ancient settlement, watching the waves rolling across the boulder field with increasing anxiety. I've never walked out this way before and didn't realise the shoreline boulders were so big. How one actually gets out to the waves off the point is also a complete mystery.

After skirting the coast for 10 minutes Mark stops and declares "We'll go in from here," before leaping from boulder to boulder like a gazelle to get down to the water's edge. Jen and me follow him. She's clearly as fit as he is, but I feel bulky, slow and clumsy in comparison to the pair of them. I also suddenly need to pee and discretely unload the contents of my bladder into my new wetsuit booties while Jen and Mark sort out their gear on top of a couple of enormous, slabby rocks.

The sea is colliding loudly with the nearby headland in a regular boom-hiss pattern and there's no let up in the lines of waves wrapping around the rocky point. I'm saying very little as I attach my leash to my right ankle and fidget with my gloves and the neck of my wetsuit.

Before I can sound him out on what we're supposed to do, Mark's off, skipping over slippery rocks down to the water's edge. I watch wide-eyed as he throws himself and his board into the swirling white water and begins paddling flat out. He gets washed off his board a couple of times, but before long he's making good progress, clearing the foam and cruising out to the shoulder of the waves a good 50 metres off shore. Jen has followed him on her bodyboard, kicking out strongly to where Mark is now sitting. He's waving at me to hurry up.

I can hear my heart beating hard in my chest as I approach the edge of the boulder field. I slip a couple of times on the slimy rocks, suddenly aware that my teeth are clenched and I'm breathing loudly through my nose. The noise from the crashing waves is deafening as I wade into the shallows, slipping and falling over submerged boulders, pushing my board ahead of me. I've lost sight of Mark and Jen and now it's just me and the sea and that soundtrack of white noise. I have no idea what to do next, but figure getting on the board and paddling would probably be a good start.

And then I'm underway. Eyes like saucers and arms flailing ineffectually, I paddle for all I'm worth, getting sideswiped by a couple of medium-sized waves but staying on board. I top the shoulder of a wave and see that Mark and Jen are even further away, almost parallel with the headland and right on the edge of the bay.

Mark's waving again and I get my head down and stroke hard for where he's sitting. I feel myself paddling up the face of a wave, certain I'm going to get rolled upside down by it, but I top the crest and drop down the other side before it crumbles.

I'm already completely exhausted and have to stop paddling for a couple of minutes, overloaded with new sensations and not really aware of my surroundings. More waving from Mark and I'm off again, staying as wide as I can to avoid the breaking waves. I'm as scared as I've ever been and feel I have no right to be out here.

Sweat filling my wetsuit, I somehow make it to where Mark and Jen are sitting. I think this must be the lineup, the spot where surfers congregate to wait for a wave. We're wide of the break though, thankfully. A succession of solid overhead waves thunders past on our inside, spray billowing backwards off their crests and showering us like a tropical rainstorm. I urgently need to rest, but realise I'm now a slave to the raging currents which are continually pushing me away from Mark and Jen, both of whom seem to have no problem staying in the one spot.

I try to sit up on my board to talk to Jen, but fall off the side, like jelly sliding from a plate. Clambering back on, I opt to stay lying prone for the moment and take stock of where I fit into all this aquatic drama. For the first time I start to absorb my surroundings, still unable to fully believe I'm out here. I'm sure I'm going to end up floating off to Newfoundland, so close am I to the open Atlantic.

The current sucks me away from Mark and Jen again and I feel like I'm on an arm-powered treadmill, plodding back to where they're stationed. I try to sit up and again tip off sideways, shaking my head at my ineptitude.

Mark's enthusiasm is infectious and he urges me to paddle in closer to the rocks.

"We'll catch something in here!" he screams over the howling wind. I want to refuse, but feel I can't – after all, this is what I wanted – and I use what's left of my strength to turn around and head in towards the reef, against my better judgement. I can see rocks beneath me and I get my leg briefly snagged on some strands of kelp. I don't know much about surfing, but I'm pretty sure we're in water that's way too shallow.

Mark shouts something incomprehensible, spins his board around and drops into a paddling position with a look of complete commitment on his face. Then I see the wave. From my awestruck and terrified perspective, it's about a million times bigger than the gentle ripples I'd surfed in Caithness. It's heading skyward as if someone is rapidly lifting a long, dark blue theatre curtain straight off the seabed. There's also an alarming, boiling phenomena going on at the base of this wall of water, which captures my attention for a bit too long. At this point in my surfing career, I'm unaware that this signifies rocks just below the surface.

Taking aeons to turn around, I offer myself to the mercy of the wall that's about to collapse on my head, certain I'm going to drown. Paddling flat out gets me absolutely nowhere and the wave just sucks me up its face.

Suddenly I'm almost vertical, still on my board but looking down at boulders under inches of clear water. For a bizarre, disconnected couple of seconds, I think to myself how nice the rocks look under the surface and then I'm freefalling straight towards them.

Everything becomes a blur of muffled roaring and desperate panic. Eyes screwed tightly shut and with my oxygen-starved lungs near to bursting, I'm completely stunned by how fast I'm travelling underwater. Instinctively protecting my head with my arms, I feel my board leash stretched to what I think must be breaking point and I'm dragged leg first into the shallows.

Sunlight hits my still-closed eyes and I flail around a bit more. Putting my feet down I realise I'm actually standing on the boulder reef in water that's only up to my shins. Mark has vanished, but then I spot him about 50 metres away, ploughing back towards Jen. I don't know whether to be scared or delighted that I'm out here doing this. I feel like a surfer, and that's great, but clearly I'm not worthy of the description.

Stumbling through the shallow water, I launch my board straight onto a submerged rock. I fall off, stagger around a bit more, plunge into deeper water, paddle for a bit, and then get vaporised by another mountainous wave. This time I'm tensed up and ready for the wipeout, but the power in these waves is still ferocious. Two more waves break onto my head before I get washed clear of the shallows to begin the long paddle back to Mark and Jen. My head is splitting and I'm boiling hot, desperate for a drink of something other than seawater.

Mark continues to fearlessly paddle his way into the path of waves I have no desire to try and catch. Despite his commitment, he's not getting up on his feet on any of them and is continually slammed onto the reef.

I assume this is an off day for him, but he looks as if he's having a huge amount of fun. Jen seems less happy and says she wishes she were on a surfboard, rather than a bodyboard.

Serious exhaustion is gripping me when a group of youngish surfers arrive at the point. All equipped with fast looking shortboards, they get straight to work, effortlessly catching wave after wave.

Floundering around, unable to lift my chest and head off the board through fatigue, I feel completely inept in their presence and certain I'm getting in their way. One of them carves across the face of a sizeable wave right in front of me, while I try to get power restored like a swamped steamship about to go aground.

Gasping and struggling to paddle back to where Mark is, I decide I absolutely have to get ashore. Another wave starts breaking in front of me and there's no way I can avoid it. Just managing to turn around, I feel the wave pick me up. I'm gripping the rails – the edges of my board – as if I were hanging out of a skyscraper window and brace for impact. Through pure luck my body position on the board means I stay with it as it's rocketed at blinding speed down the coast.

I've become an integral part of the foaming, roaring mass that's steaming into the bay. My board feels alive, skipping across the surface of the water like a flat stone that's been fired from a beach by a howitzer. I'm stunned at the speed, but relieved my board actually functions. I'm too scared to try and stand up and remain mesmerized by the rate of knots I'm clocking up.

Forgetting to lean and turn left, I scream straight onto the exposed rocks of the reef to a cacophony of splintering fibreglass. The sinking feeling I get over the fate of my board is countered somewhat by my astonished delight at how fast I've just travelled.

Given I'm now in knee-deep water, I opt to scrabble out across the reef and head for dry land. Mark and Jen aren't far behind me. Inspecting my board I see that it now has a six-inch long gash on its underside, along with several small holes. A couple of the fins have been knocked loose, their edges ragged and blunted. I tell myself this kind of damage is inevitable, but I still feel saddened that my precious family gift has taken such a battering.

When Mark joins me, it's clear his board has taken a beating too, but he seems unconcerned. We walk back to the car park with Jen, talking surfing and work, finding out a bit more about each other.

I'm absolutely shattered and mildly numbed by my first outing at Skaill, unsure of how I should feel after this unexpected promotion. I'm happy, I think, but it's the same kind of shocked relief I expect you'd get after hearing your execution had been postponed.

Back at the cars I make light of my lack of fitness and inability to catch a wave.

"Wait until you're my age," I tell Mark, before he reveals he's actually a year older than me and has been surfing around a week longer than I have.

CHAPTER 7

The day out at Skaill had been a revelation. Prior to paddling out with Mark and Jen I'd viewed the bay as the final destination on my mystic quest, far off in my surfing future. Until launching myself across the boulders I'd been following my own self-imposed, fear-driven rules about where and when I could go out. Point breaks and reefs hadn't been on the agenda.

But Mark, almost as inexperienced as I was, didn't care about where he was supposed to fit on the surfing league table, nor did he give a shit about his skill level. A seasoned mountaineer and skier, he'd climbed in the Alps, Andes and Himalayas and wasn't about to let convention or common sense dictate how he should pursue his new passion for surfing. He'd learned about Skaill when he'd first arrived in Orkney a few months before we met and was straight out to the bay at the first opportunity, getting thrashed around on the

48

left-hander and putting the first of several holes in his new board.

I now had the first of several in mine too. Examining my board back at home, I was almost in tears at the amount of damage Skaill had caused. After buying a repair kit online, I obsessively fixed every ding, hole, split and dent (after watching more YouTube videos).

Mark was back on the phone a fortnight after our first session together. He regularly checked the Bay of Skaill surf forecast online and reckoned the conditions were perfect for another try. In time, I'd come to learn that Mark always wanted to go surfing, regardless of how good or bad the forecast was. 'Suck it and see' was his philosophy and it was one that would ultimately help set me free from a few of my oceanic hang-ups.

The next morning I drive round to pick him up after discovering he lives in a rented house within spitting distance of my back garden wall. Mark, who is part Italian, is going through a complex coffee preparation routine when I arrive. The smell is fantastic and he serves me a huge mug of the stuff, along with a chunk of fruitcake and a multi-vitamin pill. I learn that he's a fellow vegetarian, a fact that adds a bit more glue to our developing friendship.

Coffee transferred into a brace of large aluminium camping mugs, we load his board up on top of mine, shove the plastic box containing his wetsuit, boots and gloves into the back of the car and hit the road.

Twenty minutes later we're at Skaill. The tide's about halfway in, the cross-shore wind strong. The left-hander on the south side of the bay is big and messy. Huge broken waves and walls of white water are steaming into the point. On the north side however, the right-hander is breaking with less size and more shape. It's still way bigger than anything I've contemplated riding before and all the action's unfolding a good distance offshore.

Mark reckons we should try the right. My guts swirl at the prospect, but I unload the boards off the car and head to the bay's small public toilet block to get changed. Since our last trip, and on Mark's advice, I've bought myself a top of the range wetsuit hood. It feels incredibly tight when I pull it over my head, but I figure I'll get used to it.

Kitted up, we lock the car, hide the keys and head down onto the beach. Mark's not been out on the right before, but decides the best way to reach the break it is to employ the same reef entry tactic as we used on the left. The shoreline's different though. Instead of the boulders of the south side, the north side of the bay comprises of layers of flagstones and hundreds of rock pools.

As soon as we're below the high tide line, the rocks get slippery. We frequently fall over, swearing about the lack of grip on wetsuit boot soles. We clamber over outcrops and edge our way across a finger of rock 30 metres from the main breaking wave, which looks a lot bigger from this vantage point. White water is boiling around the edge of the outcrop and I'm not sure this is the best place to launch from. Actually, I've no idea where the best place to launch might be, but I fasten my leash to my ankle and follow Mark who is waiting for a gap in the sets. We stand there for a couple of minutes, hoping the onslaught will ease enough to let us in.

I'm starting to think we should try something different, like maybe paddling out from the beach, when Mark throws his board into the soupy white ocean and jumps in after it. He climbs on and starts paddling, momentarily grinding to a halt as his board comes into contact with the reef. The currents swirl him around, as if he's inside one of those old top loading washing machines, but he gets his head down and paddles hard for deeper water.

He's getting further and further away from me and I decide to bite the bullet and follow. Reluctantly, I drop off the side of the outcrop into the foaming water and clamber onto my board. Teeth clenched I start paddling, but can see an approaching set of waves in my peripheral vision. I claw a bit harder trying to make it to the safety of deeper water, but the currents are strong and I'm getting washed back in towards the rocks I've just departed from.

Realising I'm not going to escape, I turn my board around to face the first of the already broken waves and try to turtle roll underneath the avalanche. I'd seen this manoeuvre in a beginners' surfing book and it looked straightforward enough. Gripping the rails of my board with my hands and legs, I roll onto my back, assuming the wave will wash over me and then allow me to right myself and continue on. It worked for the guy in the book who'd emerged smiling from his turtle roll, his progress towards surfing glory unhindered.

Instead I'm transported underwater at speed, still upside down and clamped to my board like a surprised limpet. I surface far from where I started, infuriated and disorientated. More white water is heading towards me, so I haul myself back onto the board and start paddling again. Mark's nowhere to be seen, though looking west I can see some enormous overhead waves breaking around the point and assume he's underneath them.

Gasping from the effort, I plough my way out of the white water and head wide of where the waves are breaking. This time I'm more successful, reaching slightly deeper and calmer water. I'm absolutely exhausted though and stop to catch my breath. Worryingly, I now can't see properly. My vision, particularly in my left eye, is blurred and shaking my head doesn't alleviate the problem. My neck is cracking and my lower back is sore from trying to hold my chest high off the board to see where I'm going.

There's no sign of Mark either and I begin to feel very isolated. Another line of waves collapses in my path so I have to drop down and start paddling again, head spinning. My vision is now really deteriorating and I start to think I've sustained a hit on the head without noticing it. Maybe this is all physically too much for me and I'm about to have a brain haemorrhage or a heart attack, just like my late father.

After a few more minutes of dizzy clawing around, I decide I have to head for shore. My sight problem is making me feel sick and weak, but my survival instinct is kicking in and I steam on towards the safety of the rocks, panic rising in my chest.

Connecting with the edge of the reef, I undo my leash and throw my board up onto the exposed slabs of rock, not caring if I damage it. I just need to get out. I pull myself up onto the reef and slip and stagger all the way back to the beach. When I get there, I sit down on a boulder and try to catch my breath. I feel incredibly lightheaded and have tunnel vision in my left eye.

From my slightly elevated position on the beach, I can now see Mark. He's sitting wide of the break, head rotating and clearly looking for me. He spots me on shore and I wave frantically to him, convinced I'm about to have a stroke. Displaying impressive medical instinct, he drops down and starts paddling for home. Ten minutes later he's jogging across the rocks towards me.

"What's up?" he asks breathlessly, looking concerned.

"I can't see properly," I tell him. "My vision's all blurred and I feel sick. Man, I'm glad you're a doctor."

"Hmm. I'm not sure I'll be of any use to you," he says reassuringly. "Let's have a look." He peers at me in a medical fashion, asks me how many fingers I'm holding up – it's two, I think – and then pronounces me "fine."

I pull my hood off with some difficulty, an action that instantly cures my vision problem. It then dawns on me that the hood's neck seal has been too tight, cutting off the blood supply to my brain.

"Fuck's sake," says Mark, shaking his head.

With the light fading and my sight miraculously restored, we decide to call it a day. I go home to spend some time stretching the neck of my hood and fixing another series of holes in my board.

CHAPTER 8

So began my regular surfing routine. A text or call from Mark, a trip to Skaill, holes in my board, more frustration. Between January and May of 2007 I was heading out surfing at least weekly – twice a week if I'd recovered sufficiently from the previous session.

Whilst I was certainly getting fitter and learning more about the nuances of swells and tides, I still couldn't get to my feet on a wave. I was stumped. I would paddle, catch a wave, and then invariably spend too long lying prone through fear and confusion, riding out the increasingly large walls of white water.

When I did finally try to stand up, I'd either be pitched off or find the wave had lost the volume it needed to support my weight. I knew I had to get to my feet earlier, but I found Skaill's left-hander in particular too fast for my skill level and

I hated the thought of being bounced around on the reef. In other words, I was chickening out.

Mark wasn't getting many waves either, but it wasn't due to a lack of commitment. Every time we surfed, he'd sit deep inside the path of the waves, paddling for sets he had little chance of making. I lost count of the number of times I witnessed him being annihilated by massive waves from my safe position out on the shoulder of the break. I jokingly nicknamed him 'Too Deep' and myself 'Too Wide', such was the contrast between our preferred positioning at Skaill's points. Mark would nag me to come and join him in the shallower water, but my safety catch was rusted into the 'on' position.

That said, I enjoyed the experiences we had together and I was even starting to relish the rather haphazard manner in which we approached our sessions – ignoring forecasts and just going out to see what it was like on scene. Gradually, I was starting to relax a little as far as heading into thundering surf was concerned, but I was becoming more and more frustrated by the mental barrier preventing any stand up time once I was in the water. I knew that, fundamentally, I didn't want to die, but I also desperately wanted to surf and was already addicted, even if I was useless.

The other bonus of these trips was the contact I got with the local surfing crew, though understandably none of them were in a hurry to invite us out with them. It seemed there were only three or four regular and competent surfers in the islands. Dan was a commercial diver, originally from Manchester. Duncan was the only Orcadian in the crew. Steve, another Englishman, I already kind of knew from his presence as a lifeguard in a local swimming pool. They were all a few years younger than I was and vastly more efficient in the water.

There was a lot I wanted to ask them, but I figured keeping my mouth shut and not getting in their way was the best approach towards gaining acceptance. I'd watch where they sat in the lineup, where they paddled from and what tides they favoured. None of it really helped Mark and me and I was becoming increasingly convinced the regular guys saw the pair of us as a slightly comedic double-act in the water.

The closest I came to catching a wave was on Skaill's fickle beach break, one April morning. The beach, which isn't nearly as forgiving as Dunnet Bay, had a small reef in its centre, directly opposite the public toilet block and car parking spaces. A rideable wave occasionally broke over this reef, although it was very close to shore and, from what I'd seen, one had to get up and turn along its face pretty rapidly before arriving on the beach in the grip of the hefty shore break.

Despite my blank wave scorecard on the bay's points, I looked at the beach break as too lame and only an option when everything else was too big. It was ludicrous snobbery for someone as hopeless as I was, but I wanted to shake off the beach break beginner tag.

It was crisp and sunny when we arrived. A powerful late spring swell was rolling into the bay, producing 10ft plus waves on both points that even Mark considered completely out of our league. The wind was light and offshore. The tide was also on the way in, adding more muscle to the booming sets peeling around the north and south edges of the bay. The shore break, which I frequently found problematic when trying to paddle out to the right-hander, was crunching heavily on the sand, kelp and boulders at the waterline.

I have a dose of diarrhoea in the public toilets, suddenly overcome with nerves. We suit up, enjoying the first proper sunshine in weeks and I start to relax a little. Mark skips off ahead as usual, picking his way down to the shore across the steep, boulder-covered slope in front of the toilets. I follow, trying to figure out how we're going to get through the heavy shore break to reach the wave.

Mark attaches his leash and charges straight into the white water. He gets knocked back a couple of times, but battles through in typically determined fashion. I opt to walk up the beach a little, where I can see a slightly calmer section of water.

Mark's already arrived in the general area of the break as I begin what I think is a hassle-free paddle out to join him. Pretty soon I'm level with him, but 40 metres to his left. I try to paddle across to where he's sitting, but I'm still heading out towards the middle of the bay, unable to halt my progress towards Canada. This is something new. A light comes on in my head that I must be in a rip current. I have a vague recollection about one of the local surfers mentioning the rip on this side of the bay, but I'm staggered by its power. I know from my surf book research that I have to paddle parallel to the beach to break free of it, but every time I start pulling to the south, I hardly move.

I'm now becoming more aware of the massive sets steaming in around the point on the north side of the bay, while Mark's puzzled face diminishes in size. Trying not to panic, I take a deep breath and start paddling hard in a bid to draw parallel with the toilet block on the shore. It's taking forever though and I feel my strength ebbing. Mark's waving and shouting and I can just hear his voice over the shore break implosions and backdrop of roaring from the points.

"WHAT ARE YOU DOING? COME OVER HERE!"

"I'M FUCKING TRYING!"

I finally draw level with the toilet block on the shore, although I'm still 50 metres closer to the open Atlantic than Mark. I relax a little, certain I'm now free of the rip, and turn around to paddle straight towards my baffled friend.

"What were you doing away out there?" he asks when I arrive beside him, sweating and exhausted. "There's a wave breaking here. We might actually get something."

"I was in the rip. Jesus. That was a nightmare."

I'm just about to recount my battle in greater detail when Mark spins around and paddles for a sizeable wave. He vanishes in an explosion of foam, his board flicking around in mid-air while I try to shake off the pounding in my head. I'm now watching my position in relation to the toilet block with nervy intensity, keen not to find myself back on the rip current conveyor belt.

Inexplicably, Mark's now standing on the beach, looking for an opening to get back out. I decide the time's come to engage and I paddle into the path of an as yet unbroken wall of water. I have nothing left in my arms but briefly make it to my feet – waves of shock and elation overwhelming me. The board's not actually moving though, the wave having rolled underneath me. I fall off, raging at this near miss.

My next attempt is slightly more successful, at least in respect of moving with the wave. But I'm glued flat to the deck, too exhausted to try and stand up. Belly-boarding in, I'm fired straight onto the sand and then knocked on my arse by the shore break when I try to stand up. I've had enough of this and head up the slope to the toilets.

Looking down from the car park, I see Mark's back out at sea. The shore break's becoming completely unmanageable and it looks as if Mark's stuck in the rip on the other side of the reef. He has his head down and his arms are motoring against an unseen force. After 10 minutes of relentless paddling, which only serves to illustrate both his considerable fitness and pure bloody-mindedness, he's picked up by a huge collapsing brown wave and spewed onto the beach, clinging onto his board in a death grip.

I watch Mark sort himself out at the shoreline, undoing his leash and pulling strands of kelp off his legs. He's tired, but his fatigue isn't as bad as my complete exhaustion. It's been an experience, as it always is, but I still wasn't surfing and my patience with my ineptitude was reaching breaking point. I had to try something else.

CHAPTER 9

My impending 40th birthday in June of 2007 offered a possible solution. A few weeks ahead of the big day, Shona asked me what I'd like as a gift from her and David. Clearly it had to be something of significance and substance. I already had a surfboard so that was out of the picture. The previous Christmas Shona had bought me a balance board – a short plank of wood that sat on top of a roller – in a bid to help me improve my surfing. And although I could balance well enough on this equipment, I was no closer to standing up on my surfboard. And then it hit me. I needed a skateboard.

Months earlier, I'd come across a website for a UK-based company called Lush that made longboard skateboards. These were larger than standard skateboards and usually fitted with big, soft wheels for cruising around on. Some of the board graphics had a surfy look to them and further investigation on the internet suggested longboard skating could be the key to improving my surfing.

The Lush website had a board called a Makonga that was 41 inches long and equipped with large translucent red wheels. I showed the picture of the board to Shona.

"This is what I'd like for my 40th," I said emphatically.

"A skateboard? Are you absolutely sure? I mean it's a skateboard."

"Yes."

I was never more sure about anything at that point. Surfers had pretty much invented skateboarding, so it had to be a good idea.

I wasn't completely new to skateboarding though. I'd skated as a youngster, caught up in the global craze that had kicked off in the mid-70s with the emergence of California's Dogtown skateboard revolutionaries: Jay Adams, Stacy Peralta and Tony Alva. They'd turned a slightly dorky pastime into a rebellious expression of freedom, but it took until 1976/77 for the skate revolution to properly make its way to my corner of Scotland. Skateboards started appearing in toyshops and supermarkets. We saw people skating on TV and in newspapers. We all needed a board and by the summer of '77 it seemed as if every child in my district had a little orange, red or yellow mass-produced polypropylene skateboard.

Mine, a copy of the popular California Free Former deck, was orange and fitted with translucent red urethane wheels. I also possessed yellow plastic knee and elbow pads, with rainbow-striped elastic fabric sleeves. All of us had been issued with ice-hockey helmets – skateboarding's standard head protection at that time – by parents convinced this fad wouldn't last until the end of the year, but concerned enough to try and protect their investment, and our young brains.

I grew up in Leith, where the sea meets the City of Edinburgh's northern edge. There was no shortage of smooth pavements and roads on which to pursue skateboarding, but we were all inevitably drawn to the local hills. We had a couple of outstanding examples in our district with smooth surfaces and gradients guaranteed to strike terror into mothers and fathers – had they known about our exploits.

The best of the hills was a long, wide boulevard that dropped steeply down to a harbour and the main route along the northern fringes of the city. Near the bottom of the hill was an imposing old church, beyond which lay the vehicle access to a garage and a large gap in the pavement. You could jump this gap, provided you had the speed, thanks to the slightly upturned kerbstones on the approach that acted as a launch pad. It took a level of commitment most of us didn't possess. If you were skilled enough to make the jump – and we'd seen it done by older kids – you then had the problem of stopping on the other side before you flew off the pavement and ended up under a bus.

Sunday mornings were perfect for tackling this hill. The lack of traffic decreased the risks from any unplanned entries onto the road and there were fewer pedestrians around too. We could skate up and down all morning with little hassle.

And it was on a November Sunday morning that my brief skateboarding career entered a 30-year hibernation. Getting out to skate on a Scottish autumn day was a real bonus for our little band of skaters. It was crisp and dry and the only hazards were the piles of brown leaves blowing around in the breeze. Five of us had woken that day with the same intention – to bomb down the hill and make the jump at the bottom.

None of us were regular churchgoers, although we were all members of uniformed youth organisations. As such, we should technically have been taking part in the Remembrance Sunday services and parades scheduled for that morning. However, we'd somehow convinced our parents that our absence from the ranks of the Scouts and Boys' Brigade would never be noticed. We all had old relatives who'd fought in the war and were suitably respectful of the occasion, but that day we just wanted to go downhill very fast and chalk up another skateboarding milestone.

Our boldness and speed increased with each run. There had been the odd fall, but nothing drastic. None of us had yet built up enough courage to make the jump at the bottom, but we were nearing the point of no return. Confidence was high and the conditions perfect for an attempt.

I was first to give it a go, launching from the top of the hill, devoid of fear or commonsense. My flared jeans flapped in the air and for a brief moment I was professional skater Stacy Peralta – albeit a dark-haired, slightly podgy Scottish version – storming barefoot down some Californian asphalt.

Suddenly the church at the bottom of the hill started to empty and dozens of old people in grey and black woollen coats emerged onto the street ahead of me. Some of them had medals on. A few were on crutches. One clutched a huge flagpole adorned with a Union Jack. They were busy shaking hands and chattering. One by one they turned to look uphill, eyes widening.

I had absolutely no chance of stopping. Managing to blurt out a high pitched "Excuse me!" I careened into the horrified crowd, doing some super quick slalom between the scattering bodies. I was stunned at how quickly some of them managed to move.

"You little bastard! I know where you live!" The old soldier's face was cold, grey and angry as he shook his fist at me, medals rattling on his chest. I lightly connected with a few mothball-scented shoulders and burst triumphantly out the other side of the crowd, now convinced I was going to get beaten up by some old, yet still dangerous, ex-Commando.

Negotiating the by-now-less-than-Christian crowd badly messed up my speed and timing for the jump. I should have stopped, but fearing death at the hands of the veteran mob, I went for the gap. I took off, gripped the edge of my board and, for a joyous split second I was flying to freedom like Steve McQueen clearing the first border fence in *The Great Escape*.

Halfway across the gap I knew I had no chance of making it. Gravity hauled me back down. My trucks (the axle part) connected with the opposite kerb, shearing right off and bringing the board to an instant stop. I continued on, arms and legs flailing, before face-planting onto the concrete. I wanted to cry, but all I could think about was rescuing my destroyed board.

Stars wheeling around my vision, I staggered back and picked up the pieces as the first wave of elderly shock troops approached. There was a lot of shouting about 'respect' and the sound of sturdy shoes hitting pavement. The guy with the flag was purple with rage and coming at me with his pole levelled like a lance.

Tapping into the adrenalin surging around my body, I ran like the wind for home. My friends, witnessing this epic disaster from above and fearing identification and punishment through association, ran the opposite way.

And that was the end of my skateboarding. There were a few angry phone calls and parental apologies on my behalf, but what bothered me more was the fact my board was beyond repair. For weeks I would sit and study it, trying to work out how I could breathe life back into this contraption that had brought me so much joy and terror. But I never had enough pocket money to get a new one and my hints at home about a replacement fell on deaf and relieved ears. Then winter took hold, we entered 1978 and the skateboarding craze began to die out.

CHAPTER 10

I could barely contain my excitement in the weeks before my 40th. I imagined myself effortlessly cruising around on my new longboard, practising old-school skate moves I'd instantly transpose onto the waves, next time there was any swell around. It being summer, the sea had gone fairly flat, so I was aiming to get three or four months of skating under my belt before starting a new, wave-rich chapter in my life.

My son had his 10th birthday two weeks before my 40th. Picking up on my endless enthusing about skateboarding, he asked for his own board and received one from his grandmother, who'd clearly forgotten about the irate phone calls in November 1977. Naturally, it fell upon me to teach him how to use it.

So, almost 30 years after that catastrophic Sunday morning in Leith, I'm back at the top of a steep hill in Orkney with a skateboard. There are no churches at the bottom of this one though – just a sewage treatment works. The road leading to it drops through farmland at the edge of a small bay on the outskirts of Kirkwall. Technically, this road is private and belongs to the sewage works operators. That means it stays car-free at the weekends. Most importantly, it's the smoothest road surface for miles around.

Questionably, I've earmarked this steep road as the perfect place to coach my son in skateboarding. He's fully equipped with helmet and pads and has had no problems rolling around on the flat in the days following his birthday. His board is a typical modern configuration – short as a lollipop stick, with tight little trucks and small, hard, bone white wheels. It looks very different from the board I last rode, 30 years previously, but I figure the principle will be the same and confidently offer to demonstrate a hill descent to him. I'm certain skating will be like riding a bike.

With my son diligently paying attention to my lecture about staying relaxed, I stand on the board and suddenly I'm doing about 900 mph. I'm not wearing any padding, or a helmet. Nor do I have any recollection as to how to stop a skateboard. At first it's hugely exciting. I'm 10 again and my world is free of stuff like work, bills and shopping. But then it's just teeth-clenchingly scary.

The board hits a steep section of the hill and starts wobbling uncontrollably. I'm a passenger on a runaway train and I really have to get off. Steering for some grass at the edge of the road I jump, wrongly thinking I'll be able to run at the same speed I'm travelling. My feet make contact with the road, I decelerate instantly and then cartwheel over and over down the hill. For a blissful moment I feel nothing, then my whole body hurts in a way I would have had difficulty imagining before.

Remarkably though, nothing appears to be broken. I can stand, but a quick head to toe check reveals I've ripped much of the skin off my elbows and palms. My head's taken a smack and my right hip really hurts too.

I hobble up the hill, stinging like I've been dipped in boiling water and dripping blood on the road. I then see David running back towards the car and I get a sinking feeling about what's going to happen next. Sure enough, he emerges seconds later with my mobile phone. I shout at him to stop, but it's too late. He's rung Shona.

When she gets a call saying "Daddy's had an accident," she understandably panics. Thankfully, I reach him and grab the phone before she calls the emergency services. I assure her I'm fine. David is impressed with my use of an old cloth as a makeshift bandage. I tie it with my teeth and drive home to wash the road out of my skin and get a proper lecture from Shona.

I still hadn't fully healed by the time I unwrapped my birthday longboard, but I instantly forgot about the terror of my uncontrolled descent when I saw it. Next to my surfboard, it was the most beautiful gift I'd ever received. Predictably, it was the translucent red wheels I fixated upon as they were similar to the ones I'd had on my board as a child. I couldn't wait to ride on them, though I was forced to wait until my friends arrived for my 40th party that night with a helmet and a set of pads as a present.

Initially I stuck to the flat to get to grips with riding the board. It was a lot easier to control than my son's tiny board and turned deeply and smoothly. Before long I'd graduated to riding down the lower half of the sewage works hill, carving hard from side to side to control my speed. My balance improved rapidly, along with my confidence.

More significantly – and unexpectedly – was the emotional impact that riding a skateboarding had. Rolling along in the sun, I felt my perspective on the world changing. I wasn't taking on skateboarding in the same way I'd approached surfing, as a physical challenge to be mastered through the conquering of fear. I was just a 40-year-old guy on a skateboard – a complete oddity to some. To fully enjoy the purity of the skateboarding experience meant leaving all vestiges of self-consciousness behind.

How my developing skills on a skateboard might transfer into the ocean remained to be seen. The sea had gone flat for the summer, but I wasn't caring now I could ride something that felt a little like surfing. Or what I thought surfing would feel like. I'd only ridden the foam board at Dunnet in a straight line, but on my skateboard I was carving across imaginary waves and scoring endless tubes in tropical waters.

I rolled around the local skatepark for hours that summer, helmeted and fully padded up. My son would join me on his little skateboard and I began to feel as if I was reliving my childhood with a best friend. We chattered constantly about skateboarding, encouraging each other through a list of modest challenges – ride down the steep slope, ride over the flat top of the concrete pyramid structure, ride around the bottom of the quarter pipe, and so on.

Given the small population of skateboarders in the islands, the skatepark was usually empty. On weekdays, work allowing, I'd head there by myself. At weekends the place would fill with little kids on bikes, riding down the slopes and unconsciously creating a continually moving obstacle course, around which I'd carve on my longboard.

The parents of those kids were completely baffled by my presence, particularly if I dared skate without my son. If I'd walked into the skatepark naked, with a puppy on a lead and a bag of sweets in my hand, their reactions would have been less disapproving. I knew some of the mums and dads and would say hello as I rolled past, but they were generally rendered speechless by the sight of a 40-year-old man in shorts, skate pads and a helmet. Occasionally, a parent would say something about how they'd skated in the 70s or 80s, but wouldn't dare try it now. I usually offered them a go on the longboard, but it was always declined.

Before long I began to revel in the bewilderment of parents and peers, most of whom seemed to think I'd completely lost the plot. I felt rebellious for the first time in my life. Even Mark, who'd busted his ankle on a skateboard as a child, thought I was nuts and refused to give it a try.

CHAPTER 11

It was September before I had a chance to see if my summer of skateboarding had impacted positively on my surfing. I hadn't been in the water for months, bar a couple of paddles around flat bays on the east coast of the islands.

An early autumnal swell is pulsing into the Bay of Skaill. Mark's seen the forecast and thinks it's worth a look, texting me from work. By the time he's finished with patients and ready to go, it's getting on for 6pm.

When we arrive at Skaill, the overcast sky is darkening and the wind increasing. Sure enough, there are waves breaking on the left hand side of the bay. From the shore, they look a little messy, but manageable. There's not another soul around.

We walk out past Skara Brae to the point, the sound of the surf intensifying and making my heart beat faster. Mark's in a hurry, as usual, making enthusiastic noises about the waves and how we're bound to catch 'something'.

The tide's dropping though, exposing the boulder reef and the headland looks more menacing than usual in the fading light. I'd forgotten how much this side of the bay intimidates me. Mark, not intimidated in the slightest, drops his board bag on a flat boulder and unzips it.

I note that his board has a puncture in its rail that's the size of a 50p piece. There's also a fin hanging off.

"Yeah, I must fix that," he says, pushing the fin back into place, but clearly not bothered. He bounds off across the boulders to the water's edge with his board under his arm. The waves rounding the headland are a solid eight feet, though they're smaller at the place Mark's about to enter. I follow more cautiously, thinking this is a stupid spot to try and get in from.

Mark launches himself onto the thin veneer of seawater covering the boulder field and strokes for the lineup. He paddles a few feet and abruptly grinds to a halt on a flat rock – it's becoming his signature move. Then he's off again, missing the usual avalanche of white water by the skin of his teeth.

Faffing around with my leash, which I'm coming to realise is a fear-driven avoidance tactic, I miss my opening and scramble back a few feet to stay clear of the breaking wave firing line. By this time Mark's a good bit offshore, out of harm's way, and clearly wondering why the hell I'm still onshore.

I see my chance and stumble out until I'm waist-deep in the swirling water. My desire to save my board from any further damage means I hesitate a little too long and I sigh as an overhead set explodes in front of me. I get knocked on my backside while holding my board over my head. The power in the waves takes me by surprise and is more significant than it has been during previous batterings. I stand up, stumble forward in knee-deep water and then fall into a deeper area. Here we go again.

Another set thunders over, driving me backwards onto the reef. I bounce along, partially submerged. Thankfully the rocks are fairly rounded, but it still feels as if I'm being punched and kicked by a gang of skinheads.

I surface, realising I'm back in ankle-deep water again. There's a lull in the sets and I wade out for another attempt, board at my side. After stumbling into a gap in the boulders I haul myself onto the board and start paddling, only to see another set coming my way. In the fading light it looks incredibly forbidding. The sky is grey. The sea is grey, and then everything is white and noisy again.

Back on the rocks, I catch my breath and have one last go at getting out. I wait for the sets to ease off, then launch again, fatigue and frustration rising. This time though, I clear the boulders, paddling furiously to escape the lines of advancing ocean.

After five minutes of desperate clawing, my shoulders are completely numb. I can only paddle a few strokes at a time before having to stop for a rest and my heavy breathing seems as loud as the waves exploding on my inside. I keep this stop-start routine up for another 10 minutes and finally spot Mark. He's way out the back, still a good 100 metres from where I am and visible only occasionally as he tops the dark grey swells.

I cannot believe the size of the waves rolling in around the headland. Adrenalin takes the edge off my fatigue and with eyes wide I start motoring north in a bid to skirt around the massive incoming sets. I squeak over a couple of big, unbroken faces, dropping down the back, only to find more heading my way. I am now officially shitting myself, but keep driving on until I arrive beside Mark who, unusually, is sitting well wide of the action.

"We probably shouldn't be out here," he says. He chuckles, but his face suggests he's actually serious for once.

"Fuck me. Look at that."

Turning our gaze west, we see there's a set coming, but it's forming a continuous line from the headland to beyond where we're sitting. We have absolutely no chance of paddling around it. A smooth rising wall, the same colour as the graphite sky, transfixes me. Indeed, I can hardly tell where the join between ocean and air is. I drop down and stroke straight towards it, driven by an overwhelming desire not to be in front of this set when it breaks. It's a counter-intuitive action, but I tell myself it's the right thing to do.

I'm paddling up and up, as if on an elevator, and turn to look back at Mark. His face is fixed in a rictus grin and his eyes have a resignation I've not seen in them before. He's still sitting upright on his board and it looks as if he's at least 10ft below me. Then I'm over the back and Mark's gone. I hear an enormous roar from down the point and just know he's getting a beating, but I have more pressing matters on my hands.

The wave is just the first of several boasting the same XL dimensions. The next few minutes are a blur during which I feel like a huge predator is hunting me down. More through luck than any understanding of the seabed hydrography, I get myself into a spot where I can scratch up and over the oncoming sets, though the increasing darkness is adding another unwelcome dimension to the whole drama. Panting heavily, I feel as if I'm in a fundraising advert for the RNLI.

Finally, the sets ease off. I turn my board around and paddle as hard as I possibly can for home, staying wide of the reef. I'm completely exhausted, but adrenalin keeps working my arms.

A couple of near misses and I'm into calmer water. I stop to look for Mark in the gloom, only just spotting the white of his board as he picks his way across the boulders onshore. I opt to keep heading straight back to the beach. It's close to being completely dark and my progress is slow. Stopping for another breather, I burst out laughing in what must be some kind of emotional release.

No doubt attracted by the noise, a big seal surfaces about five feet away from me. I yell in alarm, heart cranking up another few beats. Once I realise it's just a seal – not that it could be anything else – I start babbling away to it. The seal stays close as I resume paddling. I keep talking to it, asking what life's like for a seal at Skaill and whether it minds us coming into its environment. I even thank it for sharing the ocean with me, telling it I'm a vegetarian and pose no threat to it or its friends. In the dark though, it's hard to shake off the grumbling fear that it either wants to eat or rape me.

I haul myself up onto the beach in front of a silent Skara Brae, wondering if the occupants ever thought about riding waves. Not on nights like this they didn't.

I'm snapped out of my archaeosurf pondering by Mark's swearing as he appears out of the gloom, shaking his head.

"Fucking hell!"

"Indeed."

There's not much else either of us can say, really.

CHAPTER 12

By the winter of 2007 I was heading to Skaill once or twice a week, occasionally without Mark. I was nervy about going out alone, but his work commitments and the lack of light in the Northern Isles meant we had a brief daily or weekend window in which to surf and the timing didn't always suit a combined assault.

Flying solo forced some uncomfortable decision-making my way. With Mark, I'd always be drawn into a session, regardless of what was happening out at sea. Alone, I battled the demons of caution and self-preservation and wasn't always confident in my judgement of the conditions. To counter this doubt I tried hard to adopt some of Mark's bravado and didn't allow myself any time to overthink what I was doing. I'd roll up at Skaill, heart pounding, shit in the toilets, get suited up, grab my board, and then head out to sea as quickly as I possibly could.

Another trick goes badly wrong, note the wrist-guard for protection

*Above: Picking up
speed on the A9*

*Top Right: Skating
down the A9*

*Bottom Right: This
pic pretty much sums
up middle-aged skate-
boarding*

*Bottom Left: Dave
and David, skatepark*

bove: Glasgow Longboard Crew

right: Most skate tricks remain out
reach

ft: Feeling like a 10 year old again
Kirkwall Skate Park

ar left: Testing my creaking
oulder

p left: New longboard...check. New
elmet...check. Courage...um...

p middle: Not quite sure what
m doing.There was a skateboard
volved...

Left: Posing on day 2 of my surfing course in Fuerteventura

Top: Dave and Mark

Middle: Cold!

Below: Exhausted and reflective after being rescued in Fuerteventura

Right: Cruising along at the Bay of Skaill

Far-right: The theatre of my dreams and occasional nightmares, the Bay of Skaill

Bottom-right: Tired

Bottom-left: Popping up slowly

Below: Wired, shaky selfie after scoring the ride of my life at the Bay of Skaill

Above: Bay of Skaill. Skaill House in the background.

Below: On seal watch

Above: Passing the torch

Left: Mark, part-doctor, part-ninja

Below: Me and Mark after the neck seal incident

Above: Another wave goes by, unridden, at the Bay of Skaill's left hander

Below: The Bay of Skaill's right hander doing its thing

This empty bowels/empty mind approach meant I frequently paddled out on very big days when I should have stayed onshore, but I felt a gnawing need to be part of the drama at sea. On the days when I arrived to see the local surf crew far offshore, cresting the summit of a big swell, I absolutely had to be out there with them, even if I had no chance of catching a wave. But occasionally, when nobody else was out, I couldn't pull off the ballsy surfer act and would turn the car around and drive home, leaving perfect, empty waves unloading behind me.

There was no calm, happy medium in my surfing. I was either out when it was way too big, sitting on the shoulder, not catching anything, getting absolutely hammered and living completely in the moment – albeit in a wide-eyed and prone position – or I was talking myself into staying at home, waiting for 'ideal' conditions to try and progress. Either way, I wasn't actually riding any waves.

The low point in this increasingly complex mental conflict came on a perfect December morning in 2007. A huge clean swell – reportedly 10ft – and light offshore winds had delivered a top-level, five-star surf forecast. Mark was away on the mainland, but it was a Saturday and I knew everyone else would be out taking advantage of what promised to be a classic day. I couldn't ignore it, though I was resigned to the swell being too big again.

I head out as soon as it's light enough. The drive to Skaill under a cloudless blue sky is beautiful. A light frost covers the fields and the air is still. I drive with the car stereo turned up loud and the window down, singing along to a Rush track, trying not to think about how big the waves might be.

My stomach reels when I catch my first glimpse of what's happening at sea. Huge, perfect waves are peeling around the point on the north of the bay. I've never seen such big, clean-looking sets. The size is hard to judge, as it always is for me, but the faces must easily measure between eight and 10ft. Then I see a handful of figures in the water, cresting the shoulder of the sets, far offshore. They look tiny and unreachable. In a sudden rush of confidence, I decide I need to be out there with them and get suited up as quickly as possible.

The session starts off well enough. The gap between the sets of waves is long and I have no problems entering the water from the beach during a lull. I go as hard as I can to make sure I'll be in smooth water by the time the next set arrives and think I'm making reasonable progress. But when I stop to sit up and check my position, I can see that I have a long way to go.

The rest of the crew are still hundreds of metres away, right off the point, further out than I've ever been before. I keep going, but become increasingly conscious of the enormous amount of energy moving around under me. The ocean feels deep and charged. I feel small and weak.

Tired and sweating, I keep up my stop-start routine, measuring my painfully slow progress against a line of fence posts on the cliff top. I catch the occasional glimpse of the rest of the crew, taking off on huge waves out the back. They're bravely sitting deep and, in between the occasional heavy wipeout, catching fast, long rides that end well behind me.

Frustratingly, they effortlessly cruise past me on their way back to the action, whereas I never seem to be reaching the lineup.

My shoulders start to burn and I stop paddling again. Lying with my head on my crossed hands, breathing hard, I feel utterly depressed. Questions swirl around my mind. Why is this so fucking hard? Why is it taking me so long? Will I ever get any better? I feel fat, bulky, stiff and useless, just like I did during school PE lessons. Maybe I'll never be a surfer.

The self-loathing continues as I start paddling for the outside again. The bones in my neck are cracking as usual, and my overly tight hood is annoying the hell out of me. Despite the frosty air, I pull it off and shove it down the front of my suit, while wobbling around on my board, gasping and sweating.

The morning is starting to feel like a dream I've increasingly been having. In it I'm watching beautiful waves breaking far offshore, but I can't reach them for some ludicrous reason – my board or wetsuit is missing from the car, or I can't see a path down to the beach. There are always others in the water and I want to be with them, but I never make it.

I'm snapped back to reality when I look up and realise I'm further out than I've ever been before, right on the edge of the bay. There's now nothing between Newfoundland and me. Thankfully I'm in deep water, outside of the breaking waves. Mountains of ocean roll past me on the inside. Then I realise I'm alone out here, everyone else having caught a wave in.

My paranoia tells me they've all gone in because they don't want to be mixing it up with someone as inept as I am. I sit up, trying to regain some feeling in my arms. My left glove is split and I squeeze water out of the palm. It's a staggeringly beautiful day, but I'm disconnected from the environment, totally focused on the gash in my gloves. Sitting almost a kilometre offshore, in the midst of surfing perfection, I completely fail to realise that I've actually come quite far from my run-ins with the urchins of the Mediterranean and Algarve.

A pristine 10ft wave steams past me, but I'm bobbing around in despair, desperately wanting to be part of something, yet feeling like I'm not good enough for it, whatever 'it' might be.

Feeling despondent and lonely, I decide to head back in. Just as I'm turning for home I spot a darkening line on the horizon that signals the impending arrival of a colossal wave. Terrified, I start paddling back out to sea in a bid to get around it, but it's cleaning up everything in its path. It starts to break as it connects with the edge of the headland and I realise with sickening certainty that I'm going to get annihilated by it.

Inexplicably, I turn around and start paddling for it. My arms feel like limp spaghetti and I can't accelerate, not that I have any chance of matching the wave's speed. As the roaring increases behind me I stop paddling, grit my teeth, close my eyes and grab the rails of my board as hard as I can.

The impact is in a different category again to any previous wipeout I've experienced. Arms and legs wrapped around my board, I'm flipped end over end before my ride is wrenched away from me and I'm dragged underwater, leg first, for what feels like minutes. My arms flail uselessly behind me and I'm sure my leash is going to snap.

My eyes are still squeezed tightly shut and I really, really need to breathe. I feel the wave release me and I claw wildly for the surface, popping out into the sunshine and foam like I've been reborn. I'm trying to reel my board in, but another thundering mass of white water lands on my head and it all starts again. The hold-down is shorter this time and I surface with my heart hammering. Then a third wave unloads on me. This one rolls me closer to shore and I wearily clamber back on my board and dig for the beach, utterly dejected and thinking of quitting.

I didn't quit, but in the days following this surfing nadir, I realised I was never going to progress unless I took the difficult step of being completely honest with myself. The first stage in the process was recognising that my previous attempts at objective analysis of my surfing had failed, along with earlier forays into the darker recesses of my ego.

Physically, I knew I had limitations I needed to address. I was strong, but I still wasn't fit enough for surfing, nor did I have the flexibility needed to get to my feet quickly. My stiff lower back gave me trouble and my knees were creaky and weak. My arms and shoulders, heavy with useless, gym-generated muscle, were burning out long before I made it to the lineup.

All of that was relatively easily addressed, in theory at least. I had to change my gym routine, stretch more and lose some flab by running, swimming or cycling. I also decided I needed to practice pop-ups as much as possible to make the transition from prone to standing upright automatic. It was such an obvious course of action, but typically I'd kidded myself on that I could sort my surfing out without recourse to specific training.

Tackling my many mental hang-ups was a much harder endeavour. The simple act of popping up represented the final step to the freedom and confidence I craved, but more often than not I just couldn't take it. Leaving the relative security of my prone paddling position meant giving myself over to the ocean completely and that still scared me. I knew wipeouts rarely hurt to any extent and I could probably swim to shore if I lost my board, but my fears were much more nebulous. It was like being hunted by demons that lurked in the shadows.

Driving to and from Skaill I forced myself to try and untangle it all. Gradually, I came to the realisation that my oceanic fears probably related to the loss of my father as a child and my own role as a parent.

My dad died from a heart attack, aged 48, just before my

eighth birthday. It was a hugely traumatic experience that switched on a background hum of anxiety I'd never lost. One minute I'd been a normal, happy seven-year-old, playing with my mates and not really worrying about anything, and then I'd been instantly thrust into the adult world. I felt as if someone had punched me hard in the guts and knocked the wind out of me, permanently.

The morning my dad died, I became an observer of life, rather than a full participant. It removed me from the safe world I'd known, leaving me looking back at the happy, unchanged lives of my friends as if through a slightly fogged-up window. Even as an adult with good friends, a loving wife and a fantastic son, I still viewed the world from a slight distance.

When I became a father I increasingly found myself staring the old demons right in the face. I took fewer risks and planned even more, all the while worrying about the impact my own death would have on my son, and wife. I simply couldn't bear the thought of them suffering the same pain I had done as a child.

Out at sea I tried to shut out the mental picture of David and Shona living life without me, but the beach car park was fast becoming the place where I worried most about their hypothetical suffering. Often, I'd let my guard down, live in the moment and think I was finally beginning to understand the sea. Inevitably, something would then happen to chastise me – a struggle in a rip current, a beating, getting knocked on my arse by a thundering shore break. Instantly I'd be a little boy again, scared and floundering around with nobody to guide me, feeling foolish and lost. More often than not I felt just like flotsam, bobbing around with minimum influence on the outcome of the day, thinking I might at any time leave my son fatherless.

My mother and I had also moved around a lot in the years following my father's death and that unsettling experience created a deep-seated desire to be accepted. Moving from school to school had made me a social chameleon, but fundamentally I wanted the security of a close-knit group. To a certain degree, that need to belong probably explained why I was still mired in the whole surfer image thing, wanting to be part of a scene I thought was cool.

On the one hand I had a raw and completely genuine need to understand and enjoy the ocean. But still floating around on top of those deeper motivations was an attraction to the superficial lifestyle guff that accompanied surfing. The clothes, the language and the attitude – even the very action of driving around town with a board strapped to the car – it all appealed to my need for approval and admiration from others. I wanted people to know that I was now doing something special and slightly dangerous, but most importantly, I just wanted to belong to the surf community.

I was aware of all my idiosyncrasies, but never took the time to properly examine them. The ocean wasn't concerned with my fragile ego, my hang-ups and fears, or the latest line in surfing apparel. Nor did it care if I drove around town with my board strapped on the roof of my sporty Nissan SUV (with the surfing stickers on the back). The ocean was stripping absolutely everything away. Already it was showing me the harsh truth about who I was, unemotionally breaking me down into my fragile component parts. It had poured cold water on my expectations and aspirations about surfing and I was now staring into a void of raw, uncomfortable emotions. Did I want to be known as a surfer by others, or did I actually just want to surf? I was only just becoming aware of the difference.

CHAPTER 13

Death was on my mind again as I rolled into the Skaill car park on a freezing Monday morning in January 2008, though for a change it wasn't the usual tragic movie about my own demise that was playing in my head. Boxing Day had seen the passing of my 92-year-old great aunt Annie, an important figure in my life and one of those people you thought would be around forever. Her funeral, delayed until key relatives could return to Orkney after the festive season, was scheduled for the next day. The temperature was below zero, but the sky a cloudless blue. Most importantly, a clean, moderately-sized swell was rolling across the northern point of the bay.

I feel oddly calm as I suit up in the freezing toilets, taking a picture of the icicles sprouting in the urinals for my own amusement. I also feel slightly guilty about being at the beach the day before an important family funeral but I also know my great aunt wasn't one for sentimentality.

"Life is for the living." I say it out loud a couple of times as I slide across the frost-coated shoreline boulders and walk up the beach towards my entry point. The sun is shining, the birds happily doing their thing. It's peaceful and I suddenly realise my head isn't full of the usual pre-surf doom and gloom interference.

The paddle out to the point is effortless and I glide across glassy, sparkling water. The cold nips my exposed face and for once I'm glad of my stupid hood. Four-foot sets are reeling across the reef. I sit for a while to watch them, drinking in the scene around me. Then, without thinking, I paddle into the path of a perfect little wave. It lifts me, I dig in with another few strokes and then I'm moving with it. I push down, spring to my feet and I'm up, solidly planted on my board and flying.

I'm absolutely stunned and my mind is briefly shorted out with emotions. I shift my feet forward on the board and feel it accelerate along the face of the wave, which is now reforming over another section of reef, sun dancing off its surface. I try to concentrate on soaking up the view, but I can't stop looking down at my feet, my board and the blue/green liquid glass rolling beneath me.

I'm almost crying when it ends and I flop down into a prone position, wave after wave of euphoria sweeping over me. I'm laughing and shaking and it's utterly overwhelming.

"That one's for you, Aunt Annie!" I shout, feeling slightly foolish, but there's nobody else around to hear my dedication. Rather than head back out to try again, I opt to come in, such is the multi-layered significance and purity of my ride.

I'm still thinking about it at the funeral the following day, looking out across the bay beyond the cemetery and pondering how the ocean represents both life and death.

Mark was understandably sceptical when I told him I'd

actually got to my feet. Every session we had together after that January morning, I failed to catch a wave. I failed to catch them when surfing alone too, but at least I now knew it was a possibility. All I needed for a repeat was the same planetary alignment of the right sized swell and a clear, worry-free mind. Mark just reckoned I needed a larger board and bigger balls.

CHAPTER 14

Heading into the spring of 2008, my Skaill wave total remained infuriatingly at one. I didn't count the times I got to my feet for a second or two, or the occasions when I'd been stuck halfway up and ridden the board with my right knee planted on the deck. I sought the purity of a proper stand up ride and a repeat of my January pre-funeral epiphany, but was continually thwarted by bad technique and the return of my diffuse anxiety about committing wholly to the task in hand. It was if the door had been opened briefly and then slammed shut in my face.

At least my skateboarding was improving. I rode my longboard at every opportunity and was continually on the hunt for smooth road surfaces around the islands. My favourite spot remained the hill where I'd fallen while teaching my son how to skate and I'd head there any time it was dry, to repeatedly carve down from the top.

With my growing confidence came a desire to push my speed up. When the conditions were good, I'd push off as hard as I could from the top of the hill, crouch down into an aerodynamic tuck position and 'bomb' the descent at what I thought was a blistering pace. Whilst it didn't generate the overwhelming euphoria I'd got from my single legitimate ride at Skaill, it produced a nice adrenalin buzz that briefly cleared my head of worries about work, money and family.

The only element lacking from my downhill skating was company. I was aware that more people in their 30s and 40s were returning to riding, with communities of older skaters also springing up around the growing longboarding scene in the UK. But in Orkney I was still the only 40-something riding a skateboard. David was happy to join me in the skatepark, but beyond its gates I was a solo operator.

Endlessly watching skate videos online, it was clear that sharing skating with a group of friends was still as much fun as it had been when I was 10. One film in particular, *Livin' Free*, caught my imagination. It had been created by a team of American filmmakers and skaters working under the collective title of Orangfiist. I couldn't get hold of a copy of the actual film, but watched the online trailer over and over again. Beautifully shot, it documented the longboard skate adventures the group enjoyed around the USA, during breaks from their day jobs working as crew on a reality TV show. The shared experience vibe struck a chord, as did the concept of searching for perfect asphalt waves on a road trip.

It was then I decided I needed to have my own road trip, one in which I'd score long, sweeping rides down empty mountain roads, while simultaneously making friends with other Scottish longboarders.

I bounced the idea off Shona who, ever supportive, suggested we build my skateboarding odyssey into our summer family holiday. I also got in touch with the Canadian skate magazine *Concrete Wave* – the leading international longboarding publication – to ask if they were interested in a piece about my search for company. The editor, Michael Brooke, thought it was a great idea, so the trip took on a professional edge that made it all seem semi-responsible.

Before we headed off on holiday I posted up a couple of messages on internet longboarding forums, saying I was keen to meet up with anyone else riding a longboard in Scotland. The response was slow and sporadic, but I pinned down a couple of likely contacts in Glasgow and Edinburgh. It turned out that Glasgow in particular had a small but active longboarding scene, with a group of skaters meeting in the city's Kelvingrove Park each Thursday evening during the summer. I arranged to join them before heading east to my birthplace to meet the Edinburgh skaters.

Initially, the road trip plan was a bit of a washout. The first few days of the family holiday were spent in the wilds of Sutherland in rainy and windswept campsites, with zero skating. Even if they'd been dry, the local roads were largely unrideable thanks to potholes and rough, gravelly surfaces. We opted to cut to the chase and head straight to Glasgow and Edinburgh.

The weather improves as we drive down the A9 – the main route through the north of Scotland – and I decide I need to generate some material for *Concrete Wave*. A picture of me skating down a remote section of this notorious road, against a backdrop of mountains and heather, will be the perfect image for the magazine. The idea also has an appealing air of rebellion about it.

But the A9 is busy all year round, more so in the summer

with heavy tourist traffic. If I'd been undertaking the drive in the middle of the night, I might have had a chance of pulling the stunt off with some measure of safety. At 9am on a weekday morning there was a steady stream of vehicles travelling in both directions.

Fortune favours the stupid though and, just as we arrive at the top of the ludicrously steep and very wide section of the road that carves and drops around the Caithness coastline, the traffic thins out and a parking place appears.

My pads are packed somewhere in my luggage so I don't bother with them, but my helmet's easy to reach and there's a pair of leather rigger gloves stashed in beside the spare wheel. I dig out my longboard, heart racing. The occasional car goes past as I stick on a pair of skate shoes and fasten my helmet, the drivers wondering what the hell I'm doing.

"Are you really sure about this?" asks Shona, with a justifiably worried look on her face. I hand her the camera and ask her to get a few shots to record this milestone moment in my skate quest. David thinks what I'm doing is really cool and he grins with delight from the back seat of the car.

I'm feeling a little nervous as I don't have motorcycle leathers or a full-face helmet – standard wear for high-speed downhill skaters. Indeed, I'm wearing just a t-shirt and jeans, but I silence my questioning mind.

As I'm running up the hill to the launch site, I have absolutely no doubts the police around here will take a very dim view of what is probably a first for this stretch of trunk road. I'm also trying to remember where the nearest hospital is, while simultaneously not thinking about the consequences of going headfirst over the crash barrier and into the sea far below.

Another group of cars roars past, and then I'm pushing off.

90

I've no intention of bombing down flat out and start making carving turns back and forth in order to control my speed, but the incline isn't cooperating. The road's considerably steeper than it looked from the car and pretty soon I'm screaming through the Highlands, at the complete mercy of gravity. An added problem is the road surface, which is shiny and hard. My wheels can't get enough traction to enable me to turn as deeply as I need to.

Rocketing past Shona, I crouch to stick a hand down and slow myself, but that doesn't work either. I'm genuinely scared and don't want to commit to ejecting right in the middle of the road as I can see a line of traffic rounding the bend far below me.

Running out of experience and talent, I aim for a parking area on the opposite side of the road, turning hard into it and bailing spectacularly into the heather. My board picks up some minor damage but, remarkably, I'm uninjured. I drive too fast for the next five hours, shaking with adrenalin all the way to Glasgow.

I'm way too early for the evening skate session in Kelvingrove and park outside the gates looking for anyone riding a longboard. For a moment I'm paralysed by anxiety, realising I've never actually been longboarding with anyone else, let alone in such a public place. The park is within spitting distance of Glasgow city centre and there are hundreds of people around. It's pathetic given I'm 41, but I feel like I'm a little boy again, about to step into the cauldron of competitiveness that was my childhood skatepark. I no longer feel particularly rebellious.

A car rolls up and parks nearby. Two middle-aged guys and a kid of about four or five get out and start unloading several skateboards from the boot of the car. Fighting the urge to drive off, I wander over and say hello.

Charlie and Bob, as they introduce themselves, are exceptionally friendly and seem delighted to have someone else along. Between them they have six or seven boards of all shapes and sizes and, ominously, a stack of small orange cones.

"You done any slalom before?" asks Charlie, lifting the cones out of the boot.

I haven't, at least not since I was 10.

"Aye, we'll get you into that tonight then," he adds. Now I am crapping myself, thinking I've just got in tow with a bunch of serious skaters.

Pretty soon the cones are set up in a slalom course on a wide, flat and smooth area just inside the park entrance. The session just kind of evolves, with guys on longboards rolling up from all corners of the park. The atmosphere is friendly. I'm probably the oldest, but not by much.

Charlie urges me to try the slalom course he's set up, telling me how Kelvingrove Park was the venue for the 1979 British Slalom Championships. I'm not sure how that knowledge will help me, but I give it a go, miss nearly all the cones and skid out onto my backside, splitting my jeans.

There's a woman doing Tai Chi nearby, dozens of dog walkers, people on bikes, a group unselfconsciously engaged in a military-style fitness session and a guy wearing headphones doing some juggling thing. Despite the delight I feel at being seen as a rebellious eccentric back home, skating in such a public place is making me tight and nervy.

The guys are skating down a busy path leading onto the large open area in front of the park gates. All this passing humanity is totally normal to them, but I'm not used to avoiding so many pedestrians. Some are standing watching us. In time though I loosen up and realise nobody actually cares what we're doing. Nor are the guys here judging me for my lack of experience. Passers-by smile at us and there's a growing sense I'm with kindred spirits, people for whom longboarding is an actual lifestyle.

It starts to rain and the session winds up. I grab a pic of the guys standing in front of a Victorian fountain and leave with a promise to be back next time I'm in the city.

The following day I'm en route to Edinburgh to follow up a contact I got from a UK skate website for older guys called Middle Age Shred. Neil Davey has answered my plea for Edinburgh's longboarders to make themselves visible, so I'm heading through to meet him and his two friends who apparently make up the capital's entire longboarding contingent.

Neil's a 31-year-old professional photographer who has been longboarding since 2004. After getting his mail I'd checked out some of the video footage he'd posted on the internet. The clips showed some fairly high-speed technical riding, so again I found myself feeling a bit anxious about what lay ahead.

I needn't have worried. Neil and the rest of the Edinburgh crew, which consists of Dougie Brown and Stephen Cairns, are some of the most chilled guys I've ever met. Dougie and Cairnsy, as Stephen insists I call him, are both surfers in their late 20s. Cairnsy also skydives, which probably explains why he's so mellow.

We drive out of the city for about 20 minutes and into the rolling countryside of Midlothian. We take so many turns, I'm thinking we're lost, but Neil's a man on a mission and knows exactly where he's going. Eventually we hit a series of smooth backcountry roads around the little village of Temple that Neil came across by accident one day. I grew up in Edinburgh and thought I knew the surrounding countryside pretty well, but I've never been to this place. We press on for a secret skate location these guys have made their own and they promise I'm in for a treat.

We park up near a farm and a group of stone cottages. I say hello to an old guy painting a fence but he ignores me and I can hear the *Deliverance* theme tune starting in my head. Ahead of us lies a mile of perfect, winding asphalt. We all get padded up, except Cairnsy who hasn't brought any protection with him. He can't wait to get going and shoots off for a quick run down the road, pursued by Dougie.

Meanwhile, a young woman emerges from one of the cottages, followed by a cacophony of barking from what sound like very big dogs, and walks over to where Neil and me are pulling on pads and helmets. I'm thinking she's going to complain about where we've parked and feed us to her hounds, but instead she asks if we're longboarders.

It turns out the girl, called Beth, is also a longboarder. She's minus a board though, having loaned it to a friend, and we're just offering her one of our spares when Dougie and Cairnsy arrive back. Cairnsy has crashed spectacularly further down the road and ripped his brand new trousers. His arm is also badly grazed. He disappears into the cottage with Beth to get it cleaned up. It's not clear whether he's genuinely in need of first aid or just playing a sympathy card for our lovely new friend. Whatever happens inside the cottage remains a mystery, but when Cairnsy and Beth emerge she offers to pick us up after our downhill runs in her big yellow van.

After a briefing from Neil about the various turns and drops ahead, we push off and I'm treated to the most sublime longboarding experience I've ever had. Moving fast as a group, we tear through the landscape, tucking into the bends and trading the lead position. Neil comes flying past me, reminding me to stay left on the bends in case any traffic's heading our way. I nearly lose it on a steep section, but stay focused and, when we eventually come to a stop, I'm utterly charged by the purity of the run.

We turn around and head back to the top as Beth's van arrives to pick us up. Standing in the back I'm overwhelmed by a sense I've finally arrived as a skater. This collective experience is what I've been seeking.

After a couple more runs, including an adrenalin-fuelled flat-out ride on an exceptionally fast, u-shaped section of road the guys call the 'half-pipe', we head back to town. Cairnsy's very late for a sound check with his band. He doesn't drive, so Dougie has to take him to the city at an illegal rate, promising to hook up with Neil and me later on.

Neil's keen to show me a city location the crew ride whenever they're pushed for time and unable to go into the countryside. I'm finding it hard to imagine that there's anywhere quiet enough to skate in the city at this hour of the day and I'm intrigued when we roll into one of the most exclusive districts of Edinburgh. The wide steep street is framed with high stone walls and big gates, concealing the enormous homes of some of the city's most rich and powerful people. The traffic's not heavy, but the road's sited close to one of the busiest thoroughfares in Edinburgh and there are enough cars going up and down it to make me edgy. I'm also laughing and shaking my head at the pure unadulterated cheek of skating in such a location.

Neil flies off while I carve tentatively down the hill, watching out for traffic and angry rich people. A tense-looking guy in a huge black BMW drives past me, the gates to his property opening automatically and letting him sweep into his hidden driveway. We get a few odd looks from the Mercedes and Range Rover drivers, but nobody challenges us. I'm careful to avoid colliding with a top of the range Audi that's parked up on the street, though I figure I'll just run away like a kid if I do crash into it.

Dougie arrives, having dropped Cairnsy off at his sound check, and straight away he's carving hard down the street. He keeps going too, all the way down towards the junction with the main road. He skates around the oncoming traffic, ignoring the honking horns.

On my last run of the day I build up a bit more speed but it all goes horribly wrong and I'm slammed painfully onto the road as I try to avoid shooting across the junction. Then Dougie crashes too. We decide to call it a day, though I've no doubt I'll be back skating with these kindred spirits again.

I was sore, but two days amongst the longboarders of Glasgow and Edinburgh were worth the pain. I might not have skated vast tracts of the Highlands as planned, but I'd turned a metaphorical corner on my own longboarding journey.

Confidence boosted by my downhill skate experience with the Edinburgh crew in particular, I began to focus a bit more on high speed longboarding, heading out most dry evenings to push myself to go faster and faster.

Skating was no longer a vehicle to improve my surfing. So far it hadn't really done that, but I didn't care. Flying downhill on a skateboard at 30 mph was proving easier than surfing and almost as exciting.

CHAPTER 15

I may have been enjoying sticking two fingers up at social convention on a skateboard, but as far as surfing went I wasn't exactly leading the charge on a middle-age revolution. The late summer conditions had been flat though, and I focused on squeezing in as much downhill skating as I could before the weather broke, rather than seeking out any swell.

Mark, however, had been searching along the north-eastern coast of the Orkney mainland, desperate for a wave. A series of fairly marginal reef breaks ran along this stretch of coastline, out towards a high, imposing headland marking the start of the Atlantic proper.

These breaks punctuated the edge of a narrow channel between the Orkney mainland and the islands of Eynhallow and Rousay. The tides running through this channel were strong and the waves generated there during the winter were some of the biggest I'd ever seen in Orkney. Normally, we avoided the place like the plague, winter and summer, as it was way beyond our capabilities. We knew the rest of the local surf tribe frequented the area when everywhere else was flat because even the smallest of summer swells could light up a rideable wave over the reefs.

Mark had bitten the bullet first, heading out to this coastline late that summer to try and ride what looked like a small manageable wave peeling across one of the rock slab reefs. But given the height of the coastal road above the fields sloping down to the break, judging wave heights from the car was difficult. After crossing the fields and reaching the coastline, Mark realised the wave was more sizeable than he'd initially thought. Gamely taking a crack at it, he'd been thoroughly thrashed on the reef, losing a couple of fins and collecting a few more holes in his board. I wasn't sure I wanted any part of his plan to return, on a "smaller day," but thought the change of location might be the key to making some progress with my stagnating surfing.

We were well into autumn before the chance arose. On a free evening, I called Mark to see if he fancied taking a look at Skaill. He'd had a rough day at work though and, surprisingly, didn't sound too keen on heading out. Taking a lead from his normally enthusiastic self, I tried to sound charged about the forecast and encouraged him to come.

If truth be told, we were probably leaving it a bit late in the day to go surfing. Already there was a sense we were sliding towards winter, with the daylight hours this far north ebbing fast.

Mark reluctantly agrees to come, so I pick him and his board up around 5pm and we discuss our limited options for getting wet. The forecast for Skaill is nothing special, and

Mark suggests we take a trip along the north-eastern coast instead, thinking the tiny swell won't cause us many problems. I'm not so sure, but the session is my idea and I think I should just go with the flow.

We drive out in fading light and drizzle and Mark talks about his shitty day, within the constraints of medical confidentiality. Although we unwind with the miles, we have a growing sense this might be a wasted journey as far as surfing goes.

As we round the corner of a hill and get our first view down to the coast, it's apparent that the sea along here is also fairly calm. We push on regardless, knowing there's a small chance of a wave at a reef closer to the headland on the north-west corner of the mainland.

We reach a vantage point which looks down across sloping farmland to the cliffs and reef far below. There's an occasional wave coming through. We spend a couple of minutes discussing the merits of heading to Skaill, then decide it'll be too dark by the time we get there.

The temptation to turn for home is strong, but we each take a deep breath, climb out of the car and start to strip off at the roadside. The tyres of passing vehicles hiss on the wet road and lights are coming on in the houses and farms nearby. We stumble around in the mud, pulling on wetsuits, booties, gloves and hoods, knowing the discomfort we feel will be multiplied by a factor of 100 when getting changed back into our clothes.

Boards untied from the roof of the car and keys safely stashed, we head for the field we have to cross to reach the coastline. Mark says something about how the field's gate was open on his previous trip. Always trying to protect my precious board, I carefully lift it over the gate, but Mark flings his over, adding another ding to its already pockmarked surface.

The field, which slopes down to the small cliffs above the break, is incredibly muddy and the drizzle isn't helping our footing. In the twilight we can see what looks like a sketchy left-hand wave reeling across a slabby reef, close to shore.

There's a herd of cows off in the bottom right hand corner of the field, but that's no big deal. In a farming community, crossing fields full of livestock to get to a coastline isn't unusual.

The herd turns and looks at us, and then comes trotting across the field in our direction. Knowing cows to be fairly inquisitive beasts at the best of times, we're not bothered by this behaviour. But as they pick up speed we sense there's an edge to this particular welcome. I also notice these cows don't have any udders, so they're obviously male. They skid to a halt a few feet away from us and some of the bolder ones at the front of the herd start snorting and pawing the ground. All of them have a look in their eyes I've only ever seen in gangs of city teenagers wired up for dishing out trouble, or football hooligans. We quicken our pace, tension killing our conversation about the worsening weather.

The herd thunders ahead of us on a parallel course, before stopping again to stare. We draw level with them, feigning nonchalance. They again charge ahead. This bovine leapfrog game continues for a couple of minutes and we think our plan to ignore them is working. Then a crazy-looking black beast – possibly the herd equivalent of the school bully – decides to crank up the pressure. He lunges towards us and his eager mates dutifully follow in a kind of clumsy Spartan phalanx of hooves and wild eyes.

Mark and I yell in alarm and jump back against the barbed wire fencing edging the field. Our casual, rapid walk becomes a jog, but we start sliding around on the mud in our wetsuit booties – hopeless footwear for these conditions. We can now see the fence at the bottom of the field and it represents sanctuary, but our increased pace only serves to further antagonise our aggressors. Again they lunge towards us, all steam, slobber and splattering dung.

"Fuck OFF!" Mark yells, leaping around like a court jester while swinging his 7'6" board at the agitated herd. The bullocks back off a bit, before charging forward in another push. Wielding my own board like a weapon I start making cattle-herding "Yee-hah!" noises. I'm conscious that I'm also prancing around as if I was walking across hot coals rather than a field full of mud and cow shit. This only serves to further irritate the herd which is now trying to surround us in a pincer movement.

The irony of Mark and me being vegetarians isn't lost on us.

"Bastards!" he shouts. "Don't you fucking know we're your friends?"

We fight our way across the field in a ballet of flailing surfboards, slips and screams. This is turning into a Monty Python version of the Battle of Passchendaele.

Finally, we reach the safety of the bottom fence. Arms waving, I provide cover while Mark flings his board over onto the grass at the cliff top. I then do the same, catching my crotch on the barbed wire and holing my wetsuit between the legs. The herd watches us silently for a few seconds, then turns and trots back across the field, victory secured.

We catch our breath and try and prepare for the serious business of surfing, stunned and shocked by our farmland encounter. The sky is darkening now and the sea looks thoroughly uninviting. This is a very exposed spot, with strong tidal currents running in and out of the Atlantic. Typically, we can't remember which way the tide is flowing.

Before I can say, "Forget it," Mark's clambering down the cliffs, suddenly determined to shake off the hassles of the working day and our trauma with the herd. He skips across the slippery reef, launches into a channel in the rocks that's just wide of the break and paddles out into a monochrome seascape. I have no choice but to follow, as is always the way.

Mistiming my entry, I clatter across an exposed section of reef before I reach deeper water, paddling at full speed to get clear of the break. It looks much bigger now I'm in the water and it's moving very fast. Fighting the current, I eventually get to where Mark's sitting and we take a moment to reflect on our dramatic surroundings. The coast we've just launched from continues west for a couple of miles before rising up towards the headland. Then it's just wide open Atlantic.

Mark spots a bulging wall of water looming through the drizzle and starts to paddle like a madman. His eyes are wide and he's completely committed. For a moment he's in front of me, the next he's been swallowed whole by an avalanche of roaring white water. I see the tail of his board briefly exit the water and then nothing. The next time I see him he's clinging to his board in the churning foam, close to a rocky shelf beneath the cliffs. He clambers back on, turns around and begins clawing his way out of the maelstrom. A few minutes later he's back beside me, none the worse for his hammering.

"This is hopeless," he says wearily. "I think I'll go in."

I agree that we're probably wasting our time, but then we look out to sea and spot a dark grey line of swell moving in our direction. We both turn to face the shore and start motoring in a vain attempt to catch the wave, but we go nowhere, like rubber-clad hamsters on a wheel.

Seconds later we're both sucked into a giant washing machine and bounced across the reef. This being my first attempt to surf over a slab reef, I'm surprised by the ferocity of the hammering. The world goes from grey to white and I think I hear my board clattering and splintering on the slabs. When the beating eases I unfold my arms from around my head and put my feet down to find I'm in knee-deep water. I haul in my board by its leash and see that it now sports a long gash and a couple of holes.

I climb out onto the exposed reef and make for dry land, too scared to look behind me. Mark does the same. His board's lost another fin and his previously unrepaired holes are letting in gallons of water.

"Well, that was shite," he sighs, shaking his head. It's now really pouring and almost completely dark, but there's still a little light in the western sky. All we want to do is get changed and head for home, but we're now faced with an uphill walk across muddy fields, in heavy rain.

Sliding around on the wet grass and mud at the top of the cliffs, we clamber over a wooden gate into what looks like an empty field, next to the one we battled the herd in. We figure this is a wise move. Heads down, we walk quickly to stay warm, but then Mark suddenly stops dead in his tracks.

"Wasn't there a bull in this field?" he asks me.

"I'm not sure. I didn't notice on the way down. It looks empty though."

"I'm sure there was a bull in this field," says Mark, peering around for signs of life.

"Nah," I reassure him. "Let's go."

And then we spot it. There's still enough light in the sky to silhouette an object that has the dimensions of a tank but the unmistakable outline of a bull. Although motionless, it exudes menace and power. It looks up and turns its head around to see who's had the audacity to enter its territory.

"Aaah! Shit!" Recognising this adversary as being several steps up the bovine hierarchy from our earlier opponents, we head straight for the fencing at the eastern edge of the field. There's a double layer of it and we fire our boards across into the field with the bullocks. Mark grabs the wire on the first fence with both hands, and then screams.

"What the fuck?"

The fence is electrified, presumably to keep the field's enormous, angry occupant from getting out.

"Fuck, fuck, fuck! We're wearing rubber, how is this happening?"

I get shocked in the crotch as I gingerly try to straddle the fence. The bull is now turning around on the spot, like a battleship about to engage. Mark's cursing and sizzling as he negotiates the seemingly nuclear-powered fence with gritted teeth. We get over it, slide down into a ditch and clamber back up to negotiate the barbed wire of the bullock field.

By now we don't care what happens and rip a few more holes in our wetsuits. We slip and stumble all the way back up the edge of the field which is now oddly empty of curious livestock. We get changed in the dark and steady rain – an experience that's beyond unpleasant – before driving back home in silence with the heater full on.

CHAPTER 16

My heart is hammering and it would be easy to just get back in the car and drive away. Nobody would know I'd been. According to the forecast, the swell measures eight feet and it's been given a five-star classification on the Magic Seaweed surf forecast website.

I can see why. Huge, clean waves are peeling around the point on the north side of the bay. The sky is gin clear and the wind is a light offshore. Three or four surfers are in the water, sitting way out the back. They're dwarfed by the sets. Occasionally, they have to paddle wide to avoid the monster waves that jack up far out to sea and steam through the lineup in a mass of boiling white water.

The picture is unsettlingly close to that dream again – massive, perfect sets and distant surfers, too far out for me to reach. It's everything I want and yet everything I'm scared of.

It's December and I've not been in the water for weeks. I feel out of shape, frustrated, angry and weary of my constant worrying. The memory of my January ride has now faded, to be replaced by disbelief and disgust that I'm still locked up somewhere in my own head.

But soon I'm undoing the straps on my roof rack, taking the board out. I wax it up, get changed, pull on my hood and gloves and march towards the shore. It's not me though – it's someone else. I'm on autopilot, watching my rubbery legs and booties negotiate the boulders leading down to the sand. I see myself attaching my leash to my right leg, double-checking it's fastened tightly. And then I'm in the water, paddling. It's hard work, but I'm being sucked out on a powerful rip and making better progress than I expected.

The boom/hiss from the sets detonating out the back gets louder. Looking up I can see I'm gaining on the cluster of black figures rising and falling on the swell. I'm sweating inside my hood and breathing hard, but adrenalin is pumping around my body and my fear is ebbing.

I reach the lineup and take up my traditional, cautious position, well to the outside of the rest of the group. They all greet me, but attention quickly turns to the huge set that's closing out in front of us. Paddling furiously to get to the deep-water channel we sneak past it and then head back inside as soon as it's clear.

I watch the rest of the crew take turns at catching solid, clean waves. They're clustered in the same spot, well inside the firing line. The wipeouts are heavy, but the rides clearly worth the risk.

I figure I'll catch something more manageable from my position on the shoulder. It's not long before I get my opportunity. A set appears. I have surfers inside and outside of me, but nobody else seems interested in this particular wave. I've either got to try and take it, or allow it to land on my head.

Dropping into the prone position I start paddling as hard as I can. I feel myself being scooped up by the oncoming face. I get the tunnel vision I usually experience at this moment and cling onto the rails of my board as white water erupts around me.

Reluctant to relax my white-knuckle grip, it takes me forever to stand up. I do it in stages, still moving with the wave. The board wobbles a bit, but the instability stops the moment I finally stand upright. I feel the energy of the ride starting to ebb, but push forward with my left foot and I'm off again, accelerating along the wave face, stunned and delighted at the sensations of levitation and speed.

I punch the air and whoop as the ride finally comes to an end. Then I'm annoyed at myself and embarrassed by this uncool gesture. I can't help but grin though, and start the long paddle back out, heading wide and too far past the lineup. When I eventually arrive I find everyone else is gone.

Exhausted by this return trip through building surf, I make a couple of futile attempts to catch another wave. After 20 minutes of near misses, I decide to head in, satisfied I've got something to show for the day.

I'm trying to stay in line with the house on the shoreline that I use as a point of reference. It's not getting any closer though. It's also shifting to my inside and I feel as if I'm moving into the middle of the bay, despite my constant paddling. I stop for a few seconds to try and evaluate what's happening. Then I'm paddling again, breathing hard with my head down. I stop to look up and find I'm no closer to shore, with the house even further on my inside.

The rip. It's much, much stronger than it was during my

earlier experience in its grip. A wave of panic rises in my chest. Images of lifeboats and helicopters fill my mind. I can see figures up at the car park watching and wonder, briefly, if I should wave for help. I feel vulnerable and stupid, certain I'm paying some kind of cosmic price for my arrogant display of triumph after my ride.

Trying to calm down and think about what's happening, I turn the board and start heading diagonally for the car park and the shoreline audience. What I should be doing is heading the other way, towards the reef and the breaking waves as they're closer, but I want to reach those figures, urgently. I paddle hard. Stop. Paddle hard again. After 20 minutes I'm starting to really flag but then I'm free, the shoreline tantalisingly close. Another hard effort and I'm picked up by the shore break and dumped right into a massive, deep pile of stinking seaweed.

I stand up, weak from the paddling and I'm immediately knocked over by another breaking wave. The outgoing wash is sucking at my feet and board, the shoreline rocks rattling loudly like bones. I stand, take a step and sink up to my thighs in the rancid weed. Another wave knocks me onto all fours. Dignity is the least of my worries as I struggle and wade through the kelp to reach the sand, hauling my board behind me. I'm stinking of rotten weed and fish and my head is thumping from all the effort.

"You looked like a swamp monster," says one of the lads when I arrive back at the car park. I laugh it off but feel like a complete arse. I'm invited into Duncan's van for a coffee, which is a nice gesture. I'm not in the same league as him, or any of the other guys, but they're a friendly bunch and I'm delighted to listen in to their post-surf banter. I want to ask if anyone saw my one ride, but figure that would be even sadder than my battle with the shoreline seaweed and keep my mouth firmly shut.

CHAPTER 17

My surfing had certainly advanced, if one could classify a brace of decent rides over a period of two years as any kind of progress. I knew I could catch waves if I could find the guts to commit a lot more, but I was continually at the mercy of a rollercoaster of emotions. I'm sure Mark still didn't believe I'd caught anything, never having witnessed the mind-blowing rides on the right-hander that I described to him.

Most of our joint sessions took place on the left-hander and I certainly wasn't any closer to catching a ride there. Of the two breaks at Skaill, the left was the more consistent but it still confounded and scared me.

Driving to Skaill I always desperately wanted conditions to be perfect for the right, but I'd usually get to the bay to find it was the left working, with surfers out. Then I couldn't run away from it.

I would paddle out, usually from the beach, and sit wide of the break watching the rest of the local crew ride wave after wave. I tried to pick off whatever came my way out on the shoulder, but the swell hitting my favoured position invariably didn't form anything I could ride. Either that or it would steam through my spot at a completely unmanageable size, sending me flailing for deeper water.

Catching anything on the left simply required a commitment I didn't have. It was too fast and had a habit of launching me, still prone, into the clutches of the reef. My brain was just too slow to cope with its characteristics.

Mark wasn't so cautious. He frequently paddled so far inside on the left that, on low tides, he could have stood up on the reef. He often had to as he tried to extricate himself from failed attempts at taking off. His board was slowly being destroyed by his full-frontal assaults, but he didn't seem to care much.

We never got out to the lineup on the left unscathed. Going in from the boulder reef close to the point preserved energy, in theory. In practice we frequently mistimed the launch from the rocks and got rolled around for 15 minutes before battling our way through huge boulders and white water to reach the lineup. Paddling from the beach was less dramatic, though it sapped much-needed energy. By the time we reached the lineup, a good 500 metres from the beach, I'd be knackered and even less well-equipped to deal with any sets that came our way.

The more experienced local surfers bypassed all this effort and hassle by entering the water under the cliffs, almost opposite the take-off zone.

From my vantage point well outside of the break, I'd watch them making their way down to a narrow channel under the headland. From there they'd climb up onto a slanted platform of rocks where they could see waves coming around the edge of the cliffs. At the appropriate moment they'd launch into the boiling mass of an incoming swell, to be sucked back out through the rocks and into the lineup. Easy.

Taking a leap like that was almost incomprehensible for me, but the energy they saved with this instant transportation into the lineup was obvious. What concerned me most about this course of action was the fact that the biggest waves thundered right through this channel and it seemed any mistimed entry could be catastrophic.

I wasn't wrong. Turning up solo at Skaill one Sunday morning, not long after my right-hander swamp monster experience, I found the left working and a group of surfers getting suited up in the car park. Duncan and Dan were there, along with a couple of visiting South Africans.

I looked forlornly at the right hand point which wasn't doing much. The group was heading to the left so I really had no choice but to follow. We all walked out together, passing the point on the beach I'd normally have paddled from. Breaking away from the group seemed a bit lame so I stuck with them. We then passed the point on the reef where Mark and me would occasionally launch from and I knew we were heading for that ominous channel under the cliffs.

Somehow I ended up at the front of the queue, completely shitting myself but trying to play it cool. I cowered under the rock platform, peering around the edge to see if it was safe to paddle out. Set after set boomed around the headland and I had no idea how I was supposed to get out to sea.

After five minutes of this dawdling, I turned around to find Duncan and the others lined up behind me, patiently waiting to get past and up onto their entry platform. I should have climbed up there too, but instead opted to launch from where I was, without really considering if the timing was right or not. It wasn't.

As soon as I enter the channel I'm washed straight onto the rocks by an oncoming surge of white water. I stand up, stagger around, fall over, and then get hit by my board as another set unloads. This one washes me further down the point, still over the rocks.

Trying to save my board I lift it over my head, but I'm clobbered again and rolled backwards. As I stand up I can see everyone watching my progress with concerned looks. I smile vacantly and start to wade to deeper water, with my board clattering over the rocks at my side.

Another set arrives, blowing me backwards, this time underwater. I can feel my leash being stretched to its limit and I'm certain my board won't survive. My right foot gets stuck in a hole in the rocks and I'm forced onto my back, unable to stand up. Wave after wave washes over me and I'm really getting tired of this fight in what is fairly shallow water. I pull my foot free, feeling the rocks tear my boot and the leg of my wetsuit. More white water arrives and I'm off again, bouncing backwards across the reef.

Finally, the hammering ends. I've been washed well down the point and into shin-deep water. Stumbling and falling into gaps in the boulders, I make my way back towards the sea, eventually getting into water deep enough to refloat my battered board. My shins are stinging and there's water coming through the sole of my left boot.

Back at the lineup the crew are well into their session, catching wave after wave. I shake my head and laugh when I make eye contact with a couple of them, but I'm tired, frustrated and angry with myself and call it quits after an hour of fruitlessly sitting on the shoulder of the break, catching nothing.

Back on shore I inspect the damage. My lower legs are cut and bruised from being jammed into gaps in the reef and the sole of my left bootie is torn. When the rest of the crew arrive back at the car park, one of the South Africans tells me how concerned they all were for my safety. Maybe he's never seen a 220lb father get rolled across a reef before. I assure him it's just another day at the office for me and laugh it off, but I'm starting to think I'm never going to catch a wave at Skaill's left point. I'm not sure I even want to try.

CHAPTER 18

This latest beating had knocked my fragile confidence again. Subsequently, any time the left was working, I'd paddle out from the beach rather than attempt the dreaded entry from under the cliffs. The downside of this approach was, of course, being completely spent by the time I arrived at the lineup. Reluctant to commit, I fell back into my pattern of sitting wide and watching the other guys catching rides from the inside.

Frustratingly, sessions on the right-hander weren't bearing much fruit either. Despite my earlier fist-punching glory ride, I was back to a pattern of near misses, my subconscious having apparently decided I was safer not committing too much.

Doubting that my prospects in surfing would ever improve, I began to focus more attention on my downhill skateboarding. I bought a Rayne Demonseed board from a friend with a view to getting involved in the growing competitive speed boarding circuit. The board – a huge, low-riding chunk of rock hard maple – was specifically designed for speed and a rocket ship compared to what I'd been riding. It was a lot harder to control too, its back end tending to drift out on corners.

I had a couple of marginal moments on the new board, but joyously blasted down any hills I could find, relishing the speed and occasionally overtaking cars, all the while remaining oblivious to the fact that what I was doing was a lot more likely to get me killed than surfing ever was.

I skated through the summer and into the autumn, not thinking much about surfing at all. I certainly wasn't checking the surf forecast, telling myself it wouldn't be worth a look until October. In reality I was avoiding surfing, unsure of how I was going to get any better and fearful of further underwater unpleasantness.

Mark's absence was also proving a limiting factor. By now he'd moved to Australia with Jen, so as far as surfing went I was permanently on my own. My doubts and fears grew accordingly. I missed Mark enormously and felt the lack of his presence in the water acutely.

Equally, I'd become very quiet on the freelance work front. On the face of it, this might have seemed like the perfect excuse to get more water time in, but less spare cash meant fewer drives to the beach. It was just the nature of my business. I could be busy for a couple of months and then dead for weeks.

Winter came along and although I managed to score a few short and scrappy rides on the right at Skaill, surfing's significance in my life was beginning to fade.

As I entered 2010, I began to focus on how I could generate more income. Spending weekday mornings or afternoons at the beach wasn't something I could justify, either in terms of time or the cash needed to fill our thirsty 4x4 with fuel.

Weeks passed with no trips to Skaill and then two months had gone by without my having been in the ocean. Even surfing magazines and books (I'd built up an extensive library) didn't hold their former appeal.

I stayed close to home and hit the gym more often as an outlet. Lifting heavy weights once again became my focus, as it always had done when times were tough. I got bigger and less flexible, a transformation that wasn't likely to help my efforts to pop-up on a surfboard. But the gym offered me a familiar environment, one I'd always retreated to when fed up, skint or unemployed. I'd lifted weights for over 20 years and felt completely at home in gyms, regardless of where they were in the world. It was all so simple, predictable and safe.

Pouring so much energy into keeping my career alive, I simply didn't have the mental reserves to expend on butting heads with the ocean. I was weary of the fight, annoyed at my hang-ups, my overthinking, and my physical ineptitude. In the gym, I didn't experience the exhausting rollercoaster of emotions trips to the beach would inevitably generate. I was getting a regular shot of adrenalin by flying down island roads at over 40mph on a skateboard and pushing myself to progress with modest tricks in the skatepark. Maybe I no longer needed to surf. Perhaps I'd just left it too late to start and wasn't suited to an activity dominated by smaller, younger and much fitter people than me.

CHAPTER 19

Thankfully, on the professional front at least, my fortunes turned around in the summer of 2010 with a number of writing commissions and contracts appearing. There was even enough spare cash to pay for a family holiday in Fuerteventura.

I booked a surfboard for the trip, though I wasn't entirely sure I could be bothered floundering around in the Cotillo beach break again. David, now 13, was keen to have a crack at surfing and I was happy to help him progress within the bounds of my very limited knowledge.

Typically, he was up and riding the white water at the beach within 20 minutes. I tried for a few waves, but failed at every attempt, blaming the fact the hire board was too short. Truth be told, I wasn't that fussed. Weary from the previous year of work-related hassles, I was happy just to chill out, swim and snorkel, or watch my son scoring endless rides on the crumbling shore break.

Occasionally, I took the hire board out for a paddle up and down the beach for a bit of exercise. Dozens of surf school students were there every day, doing their thing. The surf school I'd signed up with five years previously was there too, but it now looked like a more professional operation. The students were all dressed in the same branded rash vests and a more attentive instructor ran up and down the beach, shouting encouragement. I paddled past them, feeling oddly aggrieved and jealous at the same time.

During the holiday I spent a lot of time swimming in a lagoon near our apartment. It was deep, warm and calm. Plodding along with my laboured breaststroke, watching the fish, I started to feel as if I was getting back in touch with the ocean again.

I began bodysurfing the Cotillo waves while David was off using the hire board, enjoying the taste, smell and feel of the sea on my body. Near the end of the second week of the holiday I was feeling fitter and a bit lighter, my fragile aquatic confidence restored to the point where I resolved that I should give surfing another chance. I also had a tan and my O'Neill baseball cap was thoroughly salt-stained. If nothing else, I looked more like a surfer than I had done in the previous five years and that was clearly still of some importance to me.

On the penultimate day of the holiday we visited the beach for one last time. The sea looked more benign than I'd seen it at any point during the previous fortnight and the lifeguards were raising green flags in the swimming area. Heading back up to their cliff top lookout station, they probably expected a quiet day.

Family beach camp set up, David took the board and headed off to paddle around. A surf school showed up, with the instructors taking a quick look at the calm conditions and departing for another location.

I decide to go for a swim as a small swell arrives, finally generating some interest for the handful of bored surfers sat on the beach. I keep out of their way, entering the water at a large sandbank, south of the flagged swimming area. There's a wave breaking across the bank and it's fun to ride it back into shore. I mess around for half an hour, and then the shore break starts getting beefier.

I dive under a couple of fairly hefty waves before catching one further out, stretching my body and arms and riding it Superman style onto the sandbank. Rather vainly, I decide this is a great photo opportunity and wade back onto the beach to get Shona to take a few shots. I feel the pull of a significant current as it runs south across the sandbank, but I'm having so much fun it doesn't register as a potential problem. On my way out, I pass a young couple paddling in the shallows, laughing and splashing one another.

Shona follows me back with the camera and I run straight into the path of the now booming shore break. Fantastic. I'm bunged full of confidence and dive masterfully under its collapsing face, pulling hard underwater. I surface and turn to bodysurf the equally large wave that's about to break behind me. I put a few strokes in to match its speed, and then I'm going backwards. I swim a bit harder but feel like I'm on a fast-moving conveyor belt heading away from the beach.

Despite knowing I shouldn't fight a rip current, particularly when boardless, fear clouds my judgement and that's exactly what I try and do. I think my gym-enhanced physical strength will overcome this situation and pig-headedly persist in swimming for shore.

It's a thoroughly foolhardy course of action, but I pour every ounce of will and power into a few fast strokes. My head is down and I'm going flat out, but I'm running out of steam and not getting anywhere. Waves are breaking over my head and I can see Shona on the shore, receding fast. She hasn't realised I'm in trouble and is shielding her eyes against the sun, taking the occasional photograph.

My head is pounding and spinning from the effort and treading water barely keeps my chin above the ocean. I have never been so exhausted. The sea is boiling around me and waves are breaking over my head. I'm a cork, unable to go anywhere.

I stop fighting it and try to calm down. Suddenly, I notice there's a young woman bobbing beside me. She's treading water and looks utterly terrified. I've got enough energy to ask her if she's okay and she nods. Then I hear a male voice bellowing in what sounds like Portuguese. It's her boyfriend and he's not happy. He's staying above the surface, but only just. He starts shouting at me and I tell him I don't understand what he's saying.

We're a good bit offshore by now, still being buffeted by waves and dragged south by the current. I know I should be swimming across the rip to escape its pull, but feel paralysed by the presence of the other people in the water. I don't know what to do. I do know I'm not a strong enough swimmer to rescue two people, yet I can't leave them. I can see Shona back on the shore and wonder if I should wave to her. She's a much stronger swimmer than I am, but I don't want to put her in any danger, nor do I want to worry her.

The young woman silently treads water, her eyes full of fear. The guy is still shouting and waving. Suddenly, he grabs my shoulders and pushes me under. He's a heavy bloke and sends me down with surprising force. It's dark. I'm running out of air.

This, it would seem, is the moment I'd feared my whole life, the one where the ocean has seen me get cocky and drop my guard. This is where I die. This is where I leave my son and my wife.

Fuck that. I claw for the surface and then the lad's back on me, still shouting, with his right arm clamped around my neck. Instinct, along with a few years of Krav Maga training, kicks in. I pull his arm away, duck under it and get behind him. He's still shouting and doesn't seem conscious of what he's been doing.

Realising we're now properly in the shit, I swallow my pride and start waving at Shona. It's then that I see a lifeguard sprinting along the shore. He stops briefly to hand his sunglasses to Shona, and then he's unravelling a tow buoy, diving into the water and hammering towards us as if he's in an Olympic freestyle final. I keep my distance from shouting guy, but feel an enormous sense of relief.

The lifeguard arrives on scene and gets the girl to take a hold of the tow buoy. Another lifeguard then appears in the water to my right, paddling a requisitioned surfboard. He deals with shouty guy. I'm still treading water, my head feeling as if it's going to explode. The young lifeguard beckons me over and tells me to grab the other side of the buoy and start kicking.

I don't want to be rescued, feeling like an idiot, but I have to admit I'm done. I willingly grab the buoy and the lifeguard sets off for shore, my kicks and feeble one-armed stroke doing little to help him. Slightly built, he doesn't look strong enough to pull two people through a monster current, but his power is remarkable. He charts a course diagonally across the current, right into an area full of hugely irritated kite surfers, but he gets us all to shore safely.

The lifeguard is called Daniel and I shake his hand and apologise for ending up in this predicament. He waves off my thanks in perfect English, adding that this kind of thing happens all the time at Cotillo. He trots off to change the green flags to red. The rescued guy and the girl wander off without saying a word to him. Later, I see them back in the shallows, messing around close to the same rip.

I spend the rest of the afternoon sitting on a rock, too drained and embarrassed to move. I downplay the whole episode to my family, but it has rattled David and he announces later on in the day that he doesn't want to return to Fuerteventura the following year.

CHAPTER 20

I felt bewildered, chastised and annoyed by what had happened at Cotillo. I'd broken all the rules – swimming outside the flagged area of the beach, not recognising the developing situation with the rip, swimming against it and not waving for help sooner. All that was technical stuff I'd seen in countless books, leaflets and videos, but I'd had to learn the hard way.

What alarmed me most was how quickly I'd been rendered completely powerless, despite years of gym sessions, the hammerings at Skaill and all the time I'd spent trying to gain some understanding of the sea. At no point in my life had I ever moved so rapidly from safety to near death and been completely unable to do anything about it. I felt exposed as a phoney waterman, vulnerable, weak and foolish – all the things I hated to feel. I was a lost little boy again, bewildered by the cold reality of life and death.

Inevitably, the experience had an impact on my planned return to surfing back home. If I'd been overly cautious before, now I was pretty much paralysed on anything other than the smallest of days. As the first autumn swells arrived on the west coast, I frequently got back in the car and headed home, creating all kinds of reasons for not paddling out.

On the days I did venture out, the slightest hint of a rip or current had me worrying about never getting home again, never seeing my wife and son. Whilst the sea hadn't killed me, it had floored me with a blow I was struggling to recover from. I never told a soul about what had happened in Fuerteventura, especially not the local surf crew. I saw less of them, choosing to paddle out solo on small crappy days, trying to repair my shattered self-confidence. Fear haunted me constantly and I began to seriously wonder if it was worth the stress. I went back to ignoring surf forecasts and tried to squeeze in a bit more skating before winter fully took hold.

But one cool October evening I took the Demonseed out for a run at my favourite spot, on the hill leading down to the sewage works. Standing at the top, pulling on my pads and helmet, I could hear what sounded like waves breaking on the east side of the headland. I'd never heard or seen waves of any significance breaking there before and figured there must be a rare easterly swell hitting the islands.

Something sparked inside of me. I jumped back in the car and headed home to check the Magic Seaweed internet forecast. Sure enough, the charts showed a decent swell coming in from the North Sea, apparently heading straight into the beach at Bu Sands, in the south east of the islands. I'd visited this wide sandy bay a couple of times, post Dunnet, on the search for a more forgiving break than Skaill, but had never seen a rideable wave there.

It's almost dark when I arrive, but the moon is up. Topping the dunes, I'm greeted with the sight of small, clean waves breaking along the whole beach. The light offshore breeze is supporting the faces of the waves, moonlight illuminating the dreamlike picture of surfing perfection.

This I can handle, probably. I feel a frisson of fear suiting up in the dunes, but know I have to do something to repair the damage done in Fuerteventura. If I don't, I'm finished with surfing. I stand on the shore for a full 20 minutes, trying to decide where to go, worrying about unseen rips and the rapidly fading light.

I finally wade out during a lull in the sets and paddle along the edge of a small reef on the north end of the beach. I feel myself being carried further north by the breeze and the current and panic engulfs me, sending me ploughing back towards the beach.

Furious with myself, I sit up on the board and try to reason this all out. The waves are tiny, the current something to be aware of, but not to be feared. I'm close to shore in shallow water. If I can't catch a wave here, then fear will be the winner and I'll spend the rest of my life endlessly floundering in a mental version of the Cotillo rip.

The swell picks up, the ocean taking on a mercurial quality in the moonlight. I turn and paddle for a wave. It gently lifts my board and then I'm on my feet, riding to the beach without thinking about anything. I drop down and paddle back out for another. The waves are small, but big enough to support my weight and they deliver countless short, glorious rides back to the beach.

I catch everything I go for and can't believe this is happening to me. I ride a wave to the shore and step off onto the sand, just trying to take it all in. The moonlight picks out the crest of a peaky wave at the far end of the bay, so I trot off and ride that for a bit before catching a few sets in the middle of the beach. It's dark by now, but the glassy waves are etched in silver and I have no trouble finding my way.

After a couple of hours the moon slides behind a cloud and I'm done. Shaking with adrenalin, I get myself changed back at the car and head home, feeling surprised and euphoric.

But tiny beach waves were one thing. Skaill was something entirely different and I knew that laying the ghost of Cotillo to rest was going to be a lot harder on Orkney's west coast. It was time to get my act together.

CHAPTER 21

As it turned out, the handful of sessions I had at Skaill in the weeks following my moonlit epiphany were fairly average. I was still carefully picking my days and hadn't entirely managed to empty my head of residue from the Cotillo rip drama. I focused, unsuccessfully, on trying to increase my wave count on small days on the right-hander and only made a couple of cautious outings on the left, again on the weakest of days. At least I was getting out a bit more. I visited the beach at Bu Sands again and again but never encountered the same conditions I'd enjoyed on that special night. I started to think the whole experience must have been a dream.

Turning up at Skaill on an overcast but calm November afternoon, I saw the left was working, properly. It didn't look too daunting from the car park, though the point's distance from the shore and my continued inability to properly judge wave height meant attempts at estimation were fairly pointless. Crucially, there didn't seem to be any massive sneaker sets steaming through the lineup. The tide was on the way in, but still had a couple of hours to go before it reached its high point.

The urge to paddle out from the beach was as strong as ever, but this time I ignored it and kept walking, right through the village at Skara Brae, now deserted of tourists, to join the path leading to the point.

As I neared the cliffs at the headland my stomach somersaulted at the sight of the sets. They weren't massive, probably chest to head high. Big enough. Perhaps too big? There would be currents and rips. And maybe helicopters and lifeboats. I kept walking, ignoring the urge to turn back and head for the toilets. The sky and ocean were battleship grey, the cliffs a damp, earthy brown. It was a primal scene, one apparently devoid of any other life. No birds, no people.

I couldn't hear anything except the boom/hiss of the sets connecting with the headland and my own increasingly heavy breathing. I started to gingerly pick my way across the boulders leading down to the feared entry channel under the cliffs.

The noise from the ocean increased, as did my urge to evacuate my bowels. I shut everything out and, heart hammering, secured my leash to my ankle. I undid it and secured it again, and then for a third time. Sets steamed past, the channel boiling with white water. This time, however, I climbed up onto the rock platform for a better look. From this vantage point I could see what was happening at the headland and, theoretically, could time my entry better.

Before I can stop myself I'm at the edge overlooking the channel. Then I'm in the water, paddling hard through the cauldron and out into the open ocean. A set rounds the headland, but I just squeak out of the firing line, eyes wide open and motoring for all I'm worth. And then I'm clear, feeling relief and no small measure of delight at having crossed another mental barrier.

I sit wide of the lineup, just trying to work out exactly what's happening with the sets. They're consistent, peeling from deep over the boulder reef with long, rideable walls. I know that today is the day I absolutely have to commit.

Surprised by how much energy I've preserved from the channel entry, I paddle deeper inside feeling strong and reasonably confident. I don't have long to wait to test my new-found mettle. A set jacks up in my path. I turn, paddle hard and get shovelled up its face. Driving myself to my feet, rather than stay glued to the deck as I would usually, I wobble and grit my teeth for the usual punishment, but it never comes.

I feel the tail of my board lock itself into the face of the wave and I'm up and flying. I automatically start turning left, suddenly mindful of the reef ahead of me. It's a shock to see a grey wall of unbroken ocean in my path. Pressing down on my front foot, I hum across the face, utterly mesmerised by the scene unfolding around me. The wave dies and I sink with it, like a hovercraft killing its engines, and that is that. I've ridden the left.

I paddled back around the edge of the sets, laughing out loud and, predictably, almost in tears. Skaill didn't look as grey and unwelcoming any more. I tried for a few more waves, again sitting deep, but was pounded by every single one. I didn't panic though, taking them on the head, riding out the wipeouts and keeping a sense of perspective about it all that I'd lacked previously. This was supposed to be fun and it was, as long as I stopped overthinking it.

I felt as if I'd turned a corner, again, but rather than place too much significance on the day's events, I accepted my modest progress as part of a natural progression – albeit one that was taking years – got my head down and paddled for home.

CHAPTER 22

I certainly hadn't been overthinking skateboarding. I was confident at speed on my longboard and had also invested in a couple of street and pool decks (designed for riding in concrete skatepark bowls, or empty swimming pools). I rolled around the skatepark whenever I could, trying some basic tricks, falling off a lot and continuing to annoy the parents of small children.

Going downhill as fast as possible remained my main focus. I still had plans to enter some of the downhill skate competitions that took place on the mainland, once I'd invested in a set of motorcycle leathers and a full-face helmet. I also needed to master cornering, but in the meantime I continued to push the envelope in terms of how much speed I could generate going downhill in a straight line. Thirty miles an hour was easily achievable, as was 40. Serious downhill guys were doing 50, 60 and even 70 at times, but tackling those speeds without leathers and a motorcycle helmet would be nuts.

Winter inevitably curtailed my skateboarding time, whether in the park or on the local hills, but my renewed confidence at sea meant I was out at Skaill at every opportunity during December and January. Whilst my session wave count remained laughably low – I'd often catch one early on and then be hammered for the next hour – I was out there amongst it, taking a beating and not overthinking. I wasn't helping my efforts to improve by my continued obsession with lifting weights, and I remained stiff and slow out at sea, but I'd stopped worrying about drowning so much and that was all that mattered for now.

Importantly, in terms of my personal growth, I was becoming less concerned about being labelled as a surfer and was just enjoying living in the moment of the experience.

However, I did secretly enjoy being labelled as a basket case who rode a skateboard. Skating, as I'd discovered early on, was a more overtly rebellious form of self-expression than surfing. Skateboards simply annoyed people. It had been the same in the 70s when I'd first skated and it had never changed. Skaters were like pirates, slicing their own path through the golf clubs and garden centres of mainstream society. As a middle-aged man riding a skateboard in a small community, I was a shorts and hoody-wearing Don Quixote. But I loved to skate and if people thought I was on the downward spiral of a mid-life crisis, then so be it.

Waking early one January morning in 2011, I saw the sun was out and the streets bone dry. The surf forecast didn't look promising, but I worked out that the fresh wind would be on my back for a downhill skate at my favourite spot outside of town. David was soon up and about, so I asked him if he wanted to join me. I suggested he use my surfy Makonga deck to try some carving and was delighted when he agreed to come.

Out at the hill conditions are perfect. There's a stiff breeze blowing down the road and the surface is completely dry. David carves his way down from the lower half of the hill, while higher up I make progressively faster runs on the Demonseed.

I decide the conditions are ideal for a flat-out run from the top of the hill. I push off hard and, once I've rounded the right hand bend at the summit, I get myself into an aerodynamic speed-tuck position. The wind is right behind me and I'm absolutely flying by the time I hit the fastest section of the hill – a short, steep drop that boosts acceleration before the road flattens again and makes a sharp right turn into the gated entrance of the sewage treatment station. I normally scrub off a bit of speed on this flat section, either by carving the board back and forth across the road, or by foot braking. The right hand bend at the bottom is very tight and it has a rougher surface than the rest of the hill. It's crucial to lose speed before taking this corner, otherwise you roll straight into the gates of the sewage station. There are also barbed wire fences separating the surrounding farmland from the entrance road.

David is walking back up the hill and stops to watch me rocket downwards. He's beaming. I return the smile. It's a cool father and son moment, one that I make sure I store away for future reflection. I think I'm setting a great example of active 40-something fatherhood as I tear past him, the wind roaring in my ears. I hit the steep section and change up a gear. I've never gone as fast as this, but I'm in control and it feels incredible.

The surrounding farmland flashes past in a blur. The bearings in my wheels are hissing with speed when I straighten my body to prepare for deceleration. Normally the act of standing up helps with braking, but the tailwind has picked up and I'm still blasting along with 100 metres to go before the bend.

A wave of alarm jolts through me as I desperately try to put down a few carving turns, but I'm not slowing down enough. If I was a more skilled downhill rider, I could throw an emergency speed check – kicking out the tail of my board so it's travelling perpendicular to the road – but I've yet to master this move effectively. My next option is foot braking, but for some reason I opt to keep both feet securely on the board and try and take the corner. I'm not wearing any pads, or gloves, which would allow me to crouch down, stick a hand on the road and lean into the corner.

The bend is on me in seconds. I run wide, the tail of my board skidding from under my rear foot and I realise I'm heading straight for the narrow grass border between the edge of the road and the barbed wire fencing. Reasoning that hitting the fence won't be a great experience, I prepare to bail. The board hits the grass and decelerates instantly. I launch off the front, thinking I might just be able to run the energy out, but there's no chance. My feet connect with the ground for a second, and then I'm pitching forward. Automatically, I tuck in my left shoulder, confident I'll roll my way out of the fall, as I've done a hundred times before in martial arts.

There's a blinding explosion of pain and light in my head as my shoulder connects with the rock-hard ground. I feel I've been hit by a sledgehammer and flip upside down, my arm going under and across my body. Stars erupt in my vision. My legs land on the fence and I feel the barbed wire tearing my jeans and puncturing my calves.

When the drama has ended, I'm lying on my back, facing

the way I came, with my legs caught on the fence. I free them and roll onto my stomach, but the pain in my shoulder is breathtaking. My arm is numb and my fingers are trembling. I groan loudly and lie there for a few seconds more, thinking it must ease soon.

It doesn't. Standing up, I pace around in a circle, swearing and hoping the agony will ebb. I try to lift my arm and it won't move very far. I feel sick and I'm pretty sure I've dislocated my shoulder, or broken something.

My board's fine. As I push it back onto the road I notice there's a deep indentation on the verge where my shoulder has impacted. Very carefully, I step on the deck and begin to push towards David. He's skated halfway down the road, sensing something is wrong.

I don't wish to alarm him and make light of the injury, but he knows I'm suffering and puts an arm around me in a touching moment of concern. He asks if I need him to call Shona, but I say I'm ok. We make it back to the car and I use the remaining, and rapidly fading, power in my arm to drive home, painfully. We crawl along at 10mph; changing gear really hurts.

By the time I reach home my arm feels as if it belongs to someone else. It dangles uselessly from my shoulder. The first thing I say to Shona when we get into the house is "I need to go to hospital," and she knows it's bad. She helps me pull my mud-covered hoody off, an action that makes me yell in agony. And then I'm back in the car, this time as a passenger. David comes too, for moral skateboarder support.

I check in at the accident and emergency ward of our local hospital. Given it's a Sunday morning, the place is very quiet. A nurse takes me into a treatment room and asks me a few questions, jotting down my answers on some official hospital document. I see the hint of a smile on her face when I tell her how I injured myself, though commendably she says nothing.

The nurse helps me take off my t-shirt and gives me a quick examination. She says my shoulder doesn't look dislocated, but will get the doctor to check it out. I turn down the painkillers she offers as I figure the doc will have a better chance of identifying any problem areas if I'm not numbed and spaced out. She leaves me sitting in a chair, pondering my accident, while she goes in search of a doctor.

As long as I don't move, my shoulder doesn't hurt too much. There's a window opposite my seat. The view's nothing special – just the back of hospital buildings – but the sight of the sky and the occasional bird flying past makes me feel like a prisoner, robbed of my freedom. My emotions revolve from sadness about the outcome of what was proving to be a fun morning, to pre-emptive defensive indignation against the criticism I think I'm sure to get from the doctor.

He too smiles when I tell him how I injured myself. He pokes around a bit and asks me to perform a series of agonising moves in a bid to determine the root of the problem.

"I'm almost 100 per cent sure nothing is broken, but we'll send you for an x-ray to check," he says. "I think you've just torn the muscles in your shoulder."

As it's a Sunday, they have to page a radiographer to come in. Despite the doctor's optimism, the x-ray shows a clear break at the upper section of my arm and a chip of bone floating around amongst the muscle and tendons. Great. I walk back to the casualty department and wait for the doctor to check the x-ray.

"I've seen worse," he says. "It looks quite stable." With that, they stick a flimsy cotton sling on my arm and that's me.

"Don't keep it in the sling all the time," advises the doc.

Even if I wanted to I couldn't, as it does nothing to support my arm and just makes the pain worse. I remove it as soon as I get home.

"You'll be leaving the skateboarding to your son from now on then, I expect," the nurse says as they send me off.

"Probably not," I reply. "And the skateboard was mine."

CHAPTER 23

The days following my accident are a blur of pain and anger. Ordinary painkillers don't help with the discomfort in my shoulder, so I have to take a mixture of two different prescription types. I alternate between the two, but have to increase the dose to numb the agony.

I can't sleep unless doped off my head, but the flipside of the heavy dose is that I fall asleep in the afternoon. I call the TV station I've been freelancing for over the past few months to alert them of my inability to cover assignments. The news editor laughs when I tell him what happened.

Then it's off to the fracture clinic at the local hospital. I sit there with kids in leg plasters and old people in slings, still clouded in disbelief. I'm also fretting about the income I'm losing.

I'm called in to see the local surgeon and, as soon as I'm

through his door, he says, "What's a 43-year-old doing riding a skateboard?"

Here we fucking go. I'm in no mood for this and I explain, at length, that skateboarding is something lots of people my age now participate in. I also tell him I've written about skating and other so-called extreme sports, therefore I have a professional interest at stake too.

He realises he's touched a nerve and says something about seeing people longboard in his native Germany. He assures me the fracture is stable and should be healed within four weeks. I've to come back to the fracture clinic if I need to, but otherwise I should be fine.

The following month is a nightmare of pain and lack of sleep. I'm permanently spaced out on painkillers and don't feel like there's much healing going on in my shoulder. I can't lift my arm beyond my waist and pulling clothes on and off is awful.

As soon as a month has passed I decide to take some positive action and start exercising. I force my arm to lift past the pain barrier and even manage a single wobbly push-up. I head for the gym and try and figure out how I can train around the injury, or indeed through it. I deafen myself listening to loud rock music while I train, but I need every ounce of motivation to try and get my shoulder working again.

A few weeks into this endeavour I'm gaining strength and mobility in my shoulder, but the pain isn't subsiding by much. I go and see my doctor who sends me straight back to the fracture clinic.

"Skateboarding? What a stupid twit," says the surgeon – a different one this time. Although this well-respected local medic is known for her straight-talking approach, the comment stings and I'm back on the defensive about skateboarding.

I'm about to launch into a monologue on how the hospital is full of injured drunks every weekend, but she gets the picture about my lifestyle choices and becomes more sympathetic.

I'm sent for another x-ray. This one shows my overenthusiastic gym routine has 'disrupted' the fracture. What this means is, I've pulled the broken slice of my humerus out of place and I'll need to see an orthopaedic surgeon to discuss the options. Fantastic.

I'm sent to see a physiotherapist to see if he can help in the meantime. He recommends some gentle exercises to strengthen the muscles in my upper back and around my shoulder, but urges me to take it easy until the surgeon has made an assessment.

Fast forward a few weeks and I've had cortisone injections, an MRI scan and consultations with two orthopaedic surgeons, all the while continuing my own intensive programme of torture in the gym. Whilst I've regained a lot of movement and strength in my arm and shoulder, I'm still plagued with niggling, burning pain and weakness.

The first surgeon I see reckons I have a simple impingement in the shoulder, easily cured by keyhole surgery. But his colleague, who'll actually do the operation, says my scans and x-rays are showing that my supraspinatus tendon – the one that does much of the work lifting the arm out to the side – is partially detached from the top of my humerus. He tells me their plan is to open up my shoulder, cut the remaining healthy tendon away, use a bone graft to fill what he describes as a "divot" in my humerus, and then finally re-anchor the entire tendon to the bone.

The surgeon won't go as far as telling me I absolutely have to get the surgery however, and says it's up to me to decide whether I can live with the discomfort. If I do get the surgery then I can expect to be out of action for months, following a strict programme of rehabilitation. There'll be no gym, no skateboarding and certainly no surfing.

It's not a hugely appealing prospect. I also have a nagging doubt over whether a reattached tendon would be any more robust than whatever connective tissue I currently have left within my shoulder.

In the end it's Mark, via a Skype call from his new home in Australia, who suggests that my current mobility and gradually increasing strength is an indication that I can perhaps live without surgery. I tell the surgeon to take me off the waiting list and then get back to the gym.

I also desperately hoped I'd get back in the water, but accepted it might take a bit of time. And whilst it seemed ludicrous to everyone but me to even think about skating again, I knew I had to get back on four wheels at the earliest opportunity.

CHAPTER 24

As I took my skateboard out of the car and set it on the ground I had one of those worst case scenario mental movies play through my head. In it, I had landed heavily on my injured arm and shoulder and was back at the hospital in agony, explaining to the doctors why I'd chosen to continue down this path in life.

I could see myself sitting inside on a sunny summer's day, arm in a sling and shoveling painkillers down my throat. My skateboard bearings would rust and my wetsuit perish. Unable to type, I'd fade into journalistic obscurity. I'd have to make a living touring schools and warning kids of the dangers of having too much fun as an adult, dressed sensibly like one of those actors in funeral plan advertisements for the over 50s.

Touchingly, David had vowed not to return to skateboarding until I was able to join him again. I knew there had been days when he'd wanted to go to the skatepark and I'd offered to take him there, but he refused to even enter the place unless I was at his side on a board. It was a remarkably noble gesture, one that made me all the more determined to get back to skating, sooner rather than later.

The late March weather was so perfect – clear, dry and crisp – there was really no question of us not going to the skatepark. Although my shoulder was painful and the outcome of falling on it would be grim, it just felt right. I knew the longer I left a return to skating, the more doubts about my abilities – and worries about the consequences of accidents – would creep into my mind.

The significance of my getting back in the saddle wasn't lost on David. He'd been there the day I'd fractured my arm and here he was at my side again, a relaxed and encouraging wingman for my first post-ejection sortie.

As soon as I put my feet on my board, I knew I'd be ok. I pushed past the fear, leaving its dark presence at the skatepark gates. In the gym I'd been physically testing my injured body, seeing what worked and what didn't. Here in the skatepark I was again running through a checklist, but this time it was entirely mental. I acknowledged the need to not fall on my left side, but otherwise my mind was clear. I also accepted that it might be a while before I could tackle anything too technical, but I was back riding and it was glorious. David, sensing that relatively normal service had been resumed, tore off and launched a celebratory air off the quarter-pipe.

It was then that I saw another father and son. The little boy, aged about six, was sitting in one of the bowl sections of the park, head in hands. The dad, a good few years younger than me, was clutching a bright red skateboard and talking gently to his son who seemed upset about something. I thought he might have fallen, or simply be refusing to go home after his session.

As I rolled past them, the father stopped me and asked if I thought his little boy's skateboard was ok. He explained that his son had seen people skating and had bought the board with his Christmas money. But now, on his first proper dry day outing, he was upset because he couldn't ride or steer it.

I took a look at the board, which was actually a really nice choice for a first deck, and explained how he could make it easier to turn. The dad then confessed that he didn't know anything about skating and wasn't sure how to coach his son. I was happy to give him some advice, but what impressed me more than anything was the fact this guy actually asked for help. I've seen so many fathers who, in a bid to save face, will crash on, regardless of the need to get proper tuition for their kids.

Granted, skateboarding is something you generally learn with peers through trial and error, but six is very young to be tackling it on your own. I told the dad how long it took to become confident on a skateboard and showed him how to stand and push, so he could then demonstrate to his son. I also assured the tearful little boy that his board was fantastic and would certainly do the job.

If we'd been in Hollywood, the little boy would have got back on his board and started to experience what it was like to skate for the first time, accompanied by a Coldplay track. But his confidence was gone and he wanted to go home. He looked defeated. His skateboard no longer represented fun and excitement, but rather something difficult, frustrating and scary. I wanted to tell him that I'd been scared by all manner of things over the years, with surfing and skating high on the list, but all I could say to his dad was "The best things are always the hardest to learn." I didn't tell them about my fracture.

Once they'd left the park, David rolled up to where I was standing and said, "I hope he comes back." I hoped he would too.

Perhaps I'll meet him in the accident and emergency room of a hospital one day and he'll blame me for ruining his chances of ever becoming Prime Minister.

CHAPTER 25

Despite the joy I felt at returning to skating, rotating my arm in a paddling motion was excruciating even without any water resistance. My fears about never surfing again were growing daily. I couldn't even bear to read a surfing magazine, or check the online forecast for Skaill, just in case I had to give it all up. I'd long since stopped flying – something I thought I'd never do – but it had become prohibitively expensive on a freelance income. I missed aviation enormously, but surfing and skating had filled the void it had left. I'd accepted that tooling around in the clouds was a thing of the past, but I was having a harder time dealing with the possibility of never finding peace with the ocean.

Whenever I met any of the local surf crew I heard myself going on about my injury, like some of the wrecked and strapped-up old campaigners I used to encounter in the gym.

Now I was rapidly becoming a surfing has-been, albeit one who'd only caught a handful of waves and never seen the inside of a tube.

The sense of panic I felt was overwhelming. I wasn't ready to walk away from surfing, regardless of how crap I was, or how slow my progress had been up to this point. It would have been easy to use my injury as an excuse to pack it all in, focus on not falling off my skateboard and spend more time doing bicep curls in the gym. I was acutely aware of my limitations as a surfer, but had come to accept them and the truths about myself that my time in the ocean had shown me.

Given I'd pretty much burned my bridges with the medical profession, I combated the problem the only way I knew how, by visiting the gym. Lying prone on a bench, I'd grab the handle attached to a cable machine and make like I was paddling. The weights I used for this simu-paddling were tiny, but my eyes watered nonetheless. I did this for weeks, alongside increasing numbers of wobbly push-ups and slow runs around town to increase my shocking fitness levels.

By the spring I felt I was ready to enter the water to see if all the agony had been worth it. I picked a weekday morning in late April for my return to Skaill. The swell was average and I figured I'd take a paddle out and test how my arm felt, without the pressure of having other surfers wondering what I was doing going around in circles.

The tide was high when I arrived and a handful of dog walkers were wandering along the shore. The sun was out, but the breeze still had a bitter edge to it. I got suited up, an act that hurt my shoulder more than I would have liked, and then pulled my board out of its bag. A chest-high wave was breaking on the right, so I carefully picked my way down across the boulders and headed for the north of the bay. I said hello to the group of dog walkers who annoyingly stopped to watch what I was doing, hands shielding their eyes against the watery sunlight.

I feel ridiculously self-conscious as I stand on the beach, slowly rotating my arms in a half-hearted attempt at warming up my shoulders. I can't wait any longer. Leash fixed to my ankle, I wade out into the shore break, convinced I'm about to deliver a glorious and defiant postscript to the saga of my busted shoulder.

As soon as I'm deep enough, I drop down onto my board and start to paddle. Instantly, pain lances my shoulder. I can't lift my chest high enough off the board and need to roll onto my right side to allow my left arm to rotate ineffectively through the water.

Thinking I just need to warm up a little more, I keep going. Progress is painfully slow, literally, as my left arm slaps the water to a soundtrack of crunching and popping from my shoulder joint.

Within ten minutes I can't use the arm anymore and feel a surge of panic about being offshore with only one functioning upper limb. The rip is pulling me out and memories of Fuerteventura come flooding back.

I sit up – which also hurts – take a breath and try to chill out. Turning for shore and angling across the rip towards the rocks, I pull hard with my right arm, using my left as rudder more than anything. Occasionally, I get the odd stroke in with it, but have little power to utilise.

Steering myself into the path of the shore break I allow it to dump me back on dry land, head thumping and shoulder tingling. The sense of relief at being back on shore is enormous, though I feel like bursting into tears as I watch the waves breaking off the point.

CHAPTER 26

I try not to think about surfing over the summer, but it's hard to shut out the sense of anger, sadness and loss I feel. It's as if I'm back looking in through the window as far as any kind of relationship with the ocean is concerned – a wounded, shore-bound spectator.

I maintained my gym sessions which were definitely working in terms of overall strength and fitness, but the issue with rotating my arm remained. I continually poked around the shoulder joint, massaging and kneading the tender area and stretched my arm every day.

Skating went some way towards filling the void. My confidence more or less restored, I spent the summer trying to progress with a series of modest tricks in the skatepark. I fell off a few times, but remembered to land on my good side. I even got some downhill sessions done, though I opted to tackle these with my old Makonga deck rather than the accident-jinxed Demonseed. Fully padded up, I kept my speed at manageable levels and avoided days when a stiff tailwind was blowing.

Over the summer I made a return trip to Temple with the longboard crew from Edinburgh, riding the hill faster than before. I tried not to think about the consequences of coming off at speed and just enjoyed the shared experience again. The following day I attempted to drop into one of the concrete pools at Renfrew skatepark and slammed horribly hard on my right shoulder in front of a crowd of kids on scooters. It hurt like hell but had the odd bonus of taking my focus off my left shoulder for a few weeks. No permanent damage was done, but it was a reminder that I was probably facing a painful old age.

It was October before I decided it was time to try and enter the water again. Hugely apprehensive, I still hurt but had a sense that my shoulder was never going to function properly unless I kept making it do what I wanted it to do. And surfing was what I wanted to do. It was what I needed to do.

Arriving at Skaill on a weekday morning, I'm disappointed to find it's the left-hander working rather than the right. It's a very small wave, peeling across the boulder reef on a dropping tide, but it'll have to do. It's a quiet morning with nobody else around. The sky is monochrome and the air has an autumnal island dampness to it.

Even though I'm alone, I feel self-conscious and clumsy getting my board out from its bag and suiting up. The gym's made me bulky and my suit feels tight across the shoulders. My heart's also hammering. For once, it's not because I'm nervous about getting wiped out. I'm just scared my fears about losing surfing altogether are about to come true.

I walk along the beach towards Skara Brae and stop under

the sea wall built to protect the ancient monument from the ravages of the Atlantic. I'm going to enter the water from the beach today, rather than risk going in from under the cliffs.

I fasten the cuff of my leash around my ankle, hesitating briefly as I try to remember what way round it goes. Once the leash is secured, I lift my board under my arm and wade out into the shallows. The water's frigid, but it smells great – clean, pure and tangy. I take a few strokes and the board moves forward. Although my left arm is taking a wider and flatter arc than my right, it's functioning okay and I've not been stopped by the blinding pain of my attempt in April.

Relieved, but still a little apprehensive, I stop-start paddle for 15 minutes before sitting up on the board. I've made it a couple of hundred metres off shore. My shoulder is warming up and aside from a dull clicking sensation in the joint it's not causing me too many problems. I still can't get my chest too far up off the board though, feeling stiff in my lower back.

I paddle around the peaky wave breaking on the edge of the reef and head out to the deserted lineup. The strengthening wind is blowing me further out into the bay and I correct my course and angle back towards the point. And then I'm in position, lined up with a cairn on the hill above the headland.

A couple of small waves come through and I try for them. My shoulder protests at the sudden acceleration and I can't get enough speed to catch them, but I don't care. It's progress. I sit up on my board and look out west to the open Atlantic, then turn around to take in the view of the bay and the shore. I have a strong sense of never having been away.

Not wishing to push my luck, I paddle slowly back to shore. It takes some effort – both of my shoulders burn and my left arm is now slapping the water a bit too often – but I'm functioning ok. Crucially, I know I'm not done with surfing just yet.

CHAPTER 27

This has to be the stupidest decision I've made in a long time. David, still only 15 and a novice as far as surfing anything other than crumbly warm water beach breaks goes, is paddling for an overhead wave on the left at Skaill, a look of pure focus on his face. I'm well outside, with a ringside seat on the unfolding drama, completely incapable of doing anything to help other than shout "paddle, paddle, paddle!" at the top of my voice. He can't hear me, though I'm relieved to see that he is paddling for all he's worth.

It's a very odd feeling watching him. I cried with joy and held him seconds after he was born, watching his tiny hand grip my fingers. Until I became a father that morning, I would never have believed it was possible to feel a love of such intensity and purity for another human being. Ensuring his welfare, happiness, comfort and survival has been my number one priority since the day he arrived.

I've learned to be a father by intuition rather than example, treasuring every moment we've spent together and worrying myself sick about him on an almost daily basis. I'd single-handedly fight the legions of hell to protect him, yet here he is, somehow, flying solo on an eight-foot swell. Furthermore, he's riding Mark's shitty old board that's been stored in my garage since my globetrotting medical friend's departure for warmer climates.

David had asked to come surfing at Skaill a few times before my accident, but it was always a step too far in my mind. I had a bad enough job looking after myself out there and throwing my flesh and blood into the mix wasn't an option.

But in the weeks following my creaky return to the ocean I realised I had to let him have a stab at it. I could have spent years telling him he wasn't ready and he'd have respected that, but it wasn't fair to let my own anxieties about his welfare influence his progress. A tall, strong lad, he was also a brilliant swimmer – way more proficient and confident in the water than I'd ever been. After a couple of drama-free test runs on small blustery winter days on the right-hander, I reluctantly accepted he was ready to start coming out more regularly.

We've turned up at Skaill on this November morning to find the left-hander absolutely pumping. My first inclination is to get back in the car and wait for a smaller day, but I remember that first trip out with Mark and decide I have to follow his example.

If David is nervous, he isn't showing it. I certainly am. Walking along the shoreline to Skara Brae I issue a continual stream of instructions about what we're going to do. I keep this commentary up as we paddle out from the beach – the channel under the cliffs can wait for now.

Typically, the waves breaking around the point are way bigger than they'd looked from the shore. I tell David to stay wide and watch what's happening. A couple of the local guys are already out, sitting close together and deep over the reef.

I just want David to get a feel for what it's like to be out here. Riding Mark's waterlogged old mini mal and dressed in my slightly too big spare wetsuit, tatty gloves and huge wetsuit boots, I'm not sure if he's going to be able to catch anything anyway.

He's paddling around on my inside when the set appears. The guys sat deep over the reef don't look as if they're going for it, but David's right in position for the clean face that's launching off the seabed.

I'm transfixed as I watch him turn and start paddling for it. He's easily six feet above me and I have a sinking feeling that he's about to get the hammering of his short life. I also feel an awful sense of dread and annoyance at myself for putting him in the line of fire like this.

And then he's gone, spirited away by some roaring aquatic pied piper. I've no idea whether he's made the wave or not as I have to paddle up and over the following set to avoid a pounding.

When everything settles down a bit I sit up and crane my neck to see where he is. The sense of relief when I spot him paddling back towards the lineup, grinning widely, is overwhelming. He's fine. Thank fuck.

I don't have any time to talk to him as I'm next in line for a wave that I'm probably not going to make. I paddle as hard as my shoulder will allow and almost get to my feet before I'm smacked off my board and propelled underwater with a force that comes as a shock after my months of inaction.

Surfacing well down the point, I'm relieved and delighted

to discover David in the water beside me. We look at each other, laugh, and then both go to duck under the collapsing face of another sizeable wave.

When he pops up, still laughing, I know he's going to be okay out here. A few more of my father/son bereavement demons laid to rest, I know I'm going to be okay too.

CHAPTER 28

Nine feet with a 15 second period, so declares the Magic Seaweed swell forecast for Skaill on Monday, 7 January 2013. The wave height is predicted to be between seven and 11ft. It sounds way too big for me, despite the fact my shoulder is now almost back to normal. The waves have been fairly consistent over the Christmas and New Year period, allowing David and me the opportunity to go out together again for a handful of fun sessions. But this day is something entirely different. I show David the forecast and he doesn't fancy it.

I load my board into the car before I have time to stop and think too much about the scale of the surf that might await me at Skaill. I doubt there'll be an 11ft wave breaking, but I still don't really know how accurate these forecasts are. And I'm still hopeless at gauging wave size. The lower end of the estimate would be more than enough for me to handle.

Skaill is deserted when I arrive. There's little wind and sea spray fills the air like fog. The left looks absolutely colossal and a complete no-go area. The right, however, is as big and clean as I've ever seen it. Huge waves peel around the point, some of them filling half of the bay. The tide is well on the way in and it looks as if getting out through the shore break could be a problem.

I watch the bay for ten minutes, trying to decide what to do. My stomach churns and I need to visit the toilets. I know if I go out alone, I could be biting off more than I can chew. But I also know that I don't really have any choice but to go. Seeing David tackle his surf sessions with confidence had, finally, diluted some of my anxiety about leaving him fatherless. I'd sorted my shoulder out and got myself fit again – for just this kind of day. Ego wasn't in the frame, nor was any stupid surfy lifestyle bullshit.

There are no other surfers out, no tourists and no dog walkers. It's just a heavy swell, a few gulls and me. Before I know it, I'm wading into the sea at the north side of the bay, having timed an entry between the remarkably predictable sets.

Paddling is hard work, but I keep my head down and motor steadily out. I have to go wide just to escape the onslaught of breaking waves on the inside. Far offshore and with one eye turned out to sea – lest a sneaker set catches me – I angle across the bay to get myself into position.

The noise around me is incredible and I sit up on my board to take stock of it all. Powerful sets roll past on my inside, spray exploding off their crests. I watch them continue, all the way to the beach. I briefly wonder if I'll ever make it home, but snap myself back to the task in hand. I feel small and insignificant, yet calm and in control. I talk to myself continually – about what I can't recall exactly – but the vibe is unrelentingly positive.

Edging my way in towards the action, I know that today is the day I'm really going to have to do this. I don't have long to wait to see if my motivational commentary has paid off.

A wave, much bigger than I'd normally contemplate trying for, has appeared on the horizon, its crest feathering in the wind. I spin around and paddle back outside to avoid the collapsing section. I keep paddling as it picks me up and feel my board slot into the face.

Then I'm on my feet in a moment akin to breaking through the clouds in an aircraft. Free of the spray, I'm thrilled to see a grey, unbroken wall of pure oceanic energy stretching out in front of me. The top of the wave is above my head so it's a completely unfamiliar picture. My attention briefly wavers and I wobble, but there's no way this is ending now. I push my front foot down and I'm off, outrunning a breaking section and picking up another boost of juice.

Time slows down. For the first time since I stepped into the ocean with a surfboard at my side, I'm able to absorb the big picture. I see the whole expanse of the bay as if I'd never seen an ocean before. It feels like the shoreline is being pulled towards me. I'm not moving my body much now, just making minor adjustments to my weight over my feet. But yet I'm travelling at light speed, finally the pilot of my own destiny.

I feel my progress slow a little, then the wave reforms over the inside reef and I'm off again. I'm stunned and delighted and never, ever want this to end. I think of the year I've just had, struggling with injury and that sense of losing touch with surfing and the ocean. I kick out just before I hit the beach, adrenalin reducing me to a mixture of tears and laughter.

Charged and hungry for more I paddle back out. I take a

succession of waves on the head which saps my energy a bit, but I also score a couple of shorter rides. In the end it's the cold that wins the day. I look at my watch and realise I've been out for almost two hours.

Chilled to the bone and starting to shiver, I head for home, feeling as if I've been connected to an IV drip full of endorphins. I stop in the shallows, slide off my board and bow to the ocean in thanks. As a tolerant atheist, it's the kind of gesture I'd once have outwardly respected but inwardly thought rather pointless. Today it feels like absolutely the right thing to do.

EPILOGUE

You probably guessed early on that this story wouldn't end with me riding a 50ft Hawaiian wave, or winning a Masters surfing contest.

I used to think it was just a cliché to talk about surfing being like a journey, but it undoubtedly is. I embarked on mine thinking there would be some kind of tangible conclusion or reward. In my case I wanted a new identity, along with knowledge, confidence and a degree of power over nature and fate.

Instead, I had the inner workings of my mind completely dismantled and then rebuilt by the sea. I was disappointed, frustrated, terrified, hurt, chastised and nearly killed. My ego was shattered. Physically, I was pushed harder than I'd ever been before. I was stripped down to the nuts and bolts of who I was, forced to actually think about what I really wanted from the ocean and my relationship with it.

Now, I'm not searching for an identity any more. If someone asks if I'm a surfer, I say I go surfing, but add that I'm fairly crap at it. I pick my days and can go weeks without being in the water, but I don't freak out about it. The ocean's not going anywhere.

When I do go out I'll often catch a couple of waves and then nothing else for the remainder of the session. On other days I'm quite happy to bob around on my board, taking in the views. Occasionally, it all comes together as it did that January day at Skaill. But generally my sessions are a mixture of comedy and bad timing, mixed with moments of unadulterated fun and pure euphoria that I never thought I'd be lucky enough to experience.

I still get scared sometimes, but accept that fear is a normal and healthy part of life and an inescapable part of the oceanic package.

Cresting a heaving, spraying wave on a cold, flinty hard day when the sea and sky are the colour of slate, or paddling as fast as my protesting body will allow to escape the looming presence of a set beyond my abilities – those are the moments I live for, just as much as the sun-dappled spring mornings when I'm gently picked up and transported across the bay by glassy waist-high surf, with only the seals for company.

Now that David has joined me at sea, I often find myself paddling along thinking of my relationship with him and the road we're travelling together through life. I'm finally at peace with my childhood loss and happy to see him embark on his own relationship with the sea.

And sometimes I just sit up and look down at my battered surfboard – an uncomplaining 7'10" chunk of foam, fibreglass and polyurethane resin. It's now starting to yellow with age and has picked up a veritable storybook of repairs. But, touched with the love of those closest to me, it's a vehicle for a voyage of self-discovery, one in which the ocean will remain my mercurial guide.

And, yes, I still skateboard.